To M
with l
for ye
family history searches.
May God bless you and may you
be a blessing to others

Virginia (Haywood)

MW01102215

RAISED BY
DIVINE
LOVE

Order this book online at www.trafford.com/07-0907
or email orders@trafford.com

Most Trafford titles are also available at major online book retailers.

Note for Librarians: A cataloguing record for this book is available from Library
and Archives Canada at www.collectionscanada.ca/amicus/index-e.html

Editor: Edna G. Markwell

Illustrator (front cover): Mark Sidney Rhodes

Printed in Victoria, BC, Canada.

ISBN: 978-1-4251-2665-0

*We at Trafford believe that it is the responsibility of us all, as both individuals
and corporations, to make choices that are environmentally and socially sound.
You, in turn, are supporting this responsible conduct each time you purchase a
Trafford book, or make use of our publishing services. To find out how you are
helping, please visit www.trafford.com/responsiblepublishing.html*

*Our mission is to efficiently provide the world's finest, most comprehensive
book publishing service, enabling every author to experience success.
To find out how to publish your book, your way, and have it available
worldwide, visit us online at www.trafford.com/10510*

www.trafford.com

North America & international
toll-free: 1 888 232 4444 (USA & Canada)
phone: 250 383 6864 ♦ fax: 250 383 6804
email: info@trafford.com

The United Kingdom & Europe
phone: +44 (0)1865 722 113 ♦ local rate: 0845 230 9601
facsimile: +44 (0)1865 722 868 ♦ email: info.uk@trafford.com

10 9 8 7 6 5 4 3 2

This book is dedicated to my husband Denis, and my late 'Mother-in-Christ' Irene Hogley

CONTENTS

ACKNOWLEDGEMENTS

THANKS GO TO many people who have been a part, knowingly or unknowingly, in my journey to Christ. Many are mentioned by name in this book, some only as a group of people who influenced me at certain times of my life. My path has crossed with hundreds of people in places such as 'Moorlands' (Methodist Guild Holidays) at Whitby, and Methodism's Cliff College in Derbyshire. In those places people have drifted into my life and out again, and although remembered for a word in season or a kindness, names sometimes escape me. For those who are not mentioned by name you know who you are and what you have done for me on that journey. To all of you I give my heartfelt thanks; you are part of what this book is about.

I also thank those who prayed about this book; who have given their advice about publishing and how finance to do so could be found; and lots of other very practical advice. Special thanks go to Edna Markwell, my friend, former Matron at Cliff College, and colleague on the Bible Society Action Group, and who has edited this book. Her teacher's grammatical accuracy, her eternal patience in correcting my many mistakes, her wise counsel on theology issues, and her encouragement have all been invaluable. Thanks to those who have tried to help with the book's cover, offering ideas, helping me formulate my own, and much more – to Krestina and daughter Ella, Ellie, Sheila, Joanne, and Margaret. My thanks would be incomplete without Mark Rhodes, professional illustrator, for being an amazing answer to prayer in doing the superb work on my book's cover. Also to Trafford Publishing, whose help and expertise and never-ending advice (even before signing up with them!) I am eternally grateful for. I highly commend both of these professionals. Were it not for a special friend in Christ whose generous-hearted gift enabled me to publish this book it would never have come to completion, and to that person I give my utmost gratitude.

My final and heartfelt thanks go to two very special people, both given to me by Jesus Christ. Irene Hogley, my late 'Mother in Christ' was all to me that a mother could be, and her prayers, her love, and her guidance contributed greatly to my 'coming to Christ' and my 'living in Christ'. Much of what she did and said, her prayers for me, and her many poems sent to help and reassure me, you will find contained in this story. Denis, as the husband given to me by the Lord, has been an absolute rock during our 20 years of marriage. When I started to write this book and during the long process of doing so he made great sacrifices by leaving our home on many occasions in order to give me the necessary peace and quiet – the solitariness – that a writer needs. In practical terms without his understanding it would not have been possible for this work to come to completion. Irene and Denis have contributed more than they could ever know to my life and my spiritual journey, and to this book which is the result of that journey.

INTRODUCTION

THE URGE TO write this book came about in several ways. For as long as I can remember writing has been as natural to me as breathing. School essays and writing projects, personal and business letters, articles for newspapers, minutes of meetings – all have been of no effort to me. People in both personal and work life have encouraged me to write. I knew long ago that my maternal grandfather, James Higginson, was a journalist, and when researching my family tree recently I noted on the 1901 census that he was also listed as a 'journalist/author'. I have yet to find out about the author part of that profession, but it fires my imagination and my desire to write even more.

This gift seems to have been handed down through the maternal side of my family. Mother's brother, Uncle Frank, son of James, was a journalist and Special Features Editor on several newspapers, and one of his daughters, my cousin Jill, trained to be a journalist. Even my mother used to write regular letters to the local newspaper on local contentious issues!

When retirement drew near I determined that I would finally put this gift to good use and researched several issues on which I felt very strongly. However when the time came that I was free to write I felt very strongly that the Lord was encouraging me to 'tell your story'. This prompt came often and in several ways, especially through the words of hymns, one of them being 'my talents, gifts and graces Lord, into Thy blessed hands receive....and let me for Thy glory live...my every sacred moment spend, in **publishing** the sinners friend' (Methodist Hymns and Psalms No 767). To many this verse of this hymn has constituted a 'call to preach God's word', and for a time I did just that as a Methodist Local Preacher until an illness curtailed my ability to do so. These words then began to take on a completely new meaning. Other prompts to tell my story came from things said in sermons, and all manner of conversations in Christian gatherings. On Radio 4's Daily Service the preacher said "If a 14 year old girl" (referring to Mary, Mother of Jesus) "can be a vehicle for God's glory, so can we". Again there was that surety that this insignificant me could be a vehicle for God's glory through my writing. Then the words from two preachers were 'one insignificant apple seed can give infinite amounts of apples' and 'one insignificant person's testimony can bear much fruit for Jesus'.

I believe passionately in testimony so decided for a time to lay aside the researched items and dedicate my time in using my family-inherited and God-given gifts to glorify God. I felt a great compulsion to tell others, through the written word, of how God had led me to Himself and had cared for me and guided me in daily life; how He raised me up from a life of sin to a life in Him with its promise of eternal life.

This book attempts to explain to the reader how God in Christ, through the power of the Holy Spirit, can take very ordinary lives and transform them. Indeed it is about how He counts as very precious those of us who consider ourselves as ordinary -even those who have taken the wrong path in life, or made mistakes. We read so much of those we term 'famous Christians', those whose books we avidly search for on the bookshelves of the library or Christian bookshops. It is often these who write of their wonderful stories of healing ministries; of powerful preaching; of powerful work through their writings. Yet God in Christ continually comes to the ordinary life and transforms it through daily acts of miracles of His grace. It is my prayer that God will use my story to bring great glory to His name and to draw others to Himself.

Read it and believe it, for His grace, His love, and His guidance is for you too.

Raised by the breath of Love Divine
We urge our way with strength renewed
The church of the first-born to join
We travel to the mount of God.
With joy upon our heads arise
And meet our Captain in the skies.

Charles Wesley, 1747

The Poetical Works of John and Charles Wesley
(London, 1869), 4:262, 263.

CHAPTER ONE

'A NEW BEGINNING'

'Behold I make all things new' (Rev 21 : 15)

I AWOKE FROM a very beautiful dream. A very vivid dream. A dream of which the details are as clear now years afterwards, despite my failing memory, as they were at the time. In my dream I very forcibly stormed out of a house, closing lots of doors behind me as I went. I then walked through a garden and into what appeared to be a conservatory, full of beautiful plants and flowers. They were exotic, and the scent was indescribably sweet. Whilst sitting alone in the midst of this beauty someone I loved dearly came in after me and told me that he loved me.

As a Christian I make no claim to the gift of interpretation of dreams for I know that such is a gift of the Holy Spirit. It is given at various times to various people, often for very specific reasons. However, as I look back on that dream it seems significant that at that particular moment in my life I had closed doors on my past life. The someone who had come after me at that moment in time, and who had told me He loved me, was none other than the Lord Jesus Christ, the Good Shepherd seeking the one who was lost. In the weeks and months that followed there would be many stages to that closing of doors of the past and I now believe the dream was what that signified. I have had no other interpretation of it but no doubt I will find out some day if it was meant to be something else.

I awoke from the dream and lifted my eyes to the chink in the rose-patterned curtains. Pale streaks began to appear in the inky sky as dawn began to break. I was intensely aware of the dawn chorus just beginning to tune up. It sounded very beautiful as the birds chirped joyously at the start of this new day.

A new day...a new beginning. It was warm and cosy in the big double bed and I was thankful to be there and to savour the warm and peaceful silence which was a part of this home. How blest I was to be here. Very soon, in the bedroom next door, I heard the 'teasmade' become active, making early morning tea for Auntie Irene and Uncle Joe. Shortly afterwards there were soft murmurs as they joined together, husband and wife, in prayer and in reading God's Word.

As I lay there cosily, with a sense of being surrounded by immense love, it was hard to believe that the past was behind me. Hard to believe that the mistakes of past years and the absolute horrors of recent months were all over. That morning the world and all within it looked very beautiful through my eyes.

God, in His graciousness, had led me to this home and these people, and here the prodigal child had finally returned home to her loving Heavenly Father. At this moment in time I was not fully aware of the significance of that nor of the work which He was still to do in me. However, here in this place, God's plan for my life gently started to take shape.

Years later I paused many a time to consider how often we impede God's plan for our lives, and to reflect on the fact that our self-willed ways often delay or impede the good things He has for us. I realised later that amongst all the magnificent facets that make up the character and nature of God is one of infinite patience with us.

Slowly, through that chink in the curtains I saw the sky lighten as this new and wonderful day burst into life. The dawn chorus stopped its full-throated twittering and quietened down to intermittent but very sweet song. As the sun arose its golden rays crept into the bedroom and began to shed its warm light onto the bedspread.

Other sounds began to pervade the house. There was the pop-pop noise of the central heating radiators as the central heating came on and they began to warm up. Then a creak of loose floorboards and soft tread on the carpets, the swish of curtains as they were pulled open in the room below me. From the kitchen I heard the clatter of breakfast pots. These were strange things to give praise and thanks for but to one who had recently lost everything in life they signified normality again.

As I looked forward to the week ahead there was indeed much to give thanks for. There was the anticipation of seeing yet again the friends of Irene and Joe – these wonderful Christians who had welcomed me into their hearts and homes. They had welcomed me – not knowing me – with a warmth and love I had never experienced before. There was great anticipation at again sharing with them at the Prayer and Bible Study Group where I would have further opportunity to listen to them delving deep into the Scriptures. There I would be helped to understand more of the Bible as I listened to their discussions and explanations. Then there would be the prayers – such beautiful and moving prayers, the like of which I had never heard before. These were prayers spoken with such love and sincerity that it was obvious these people had a very close and personal relationship with Jesus. I had never met people like these before, even though I had been baptised into the Anglican Church and later become a member of the Methodist Church. There was something different, something very special about these people, and I was very drawn to them.

As I lay there in that cosy bed, my mind wandered into the past. I asked myself why oh why had I spent all those years wandering away from Jesus? Why had it taken such a long time, 38 years, to come to this point in my life? But, I must have no recriminations. I had finally 'arrived'. I was here at last, in the place and at the time where I began to really know Jesus. No recriminations.

I guess that for many Christians there will be a 'special place', a place where they first began to know Jesus and decided to follow Him. For me it was the villages of Cookridge and Bramhope, little places on the outskirts of Leeds in West Yorkshire. The time was Spring 1981. It was a beautiful Spring, or at least that's the way it seemed to me. Perhaps I was looking at the world through new eyes? I seemed to have a heightened awareness of everything beautiful – not just the countryside surrounding the village but of the people too. There was this heightened awareness of a special kind of love in their hearts, fanned into being by the Creator of Life and Love. I wanted so desperately to be the kind of person they were. I wished with all my heart to possess that love and joy and peace that emanated from these people. They knew Jesus in a way I didn't and I longed to know Him as they did.

CHAPTER TWO

FORGET THE TIES OF THE PAST

'Do not cling to events of the past, or dwell on what happened long ago'

(Isaiah 43 : 18)

HOW? HOW COULD I become like these people? I was suddenly very aware of my sinfulness and of my past failures. I remembered a prayer from childhood...'we have erred and strayed from Thy ways like lost sheep'. And *how*. I felt convicted of sin and had a great sense as of nothingworth.

I had been brought up by very loving parents – kind, gentle, patient people, whose lives had been a great example to me. My Mother had been a quiet sincere Christian and years later I would often picture in my mind's eye the amount of time she spent on her knees in prayer, particularly at her bedside.

adoring parents

Where, with that kind of upbringing, had I gone wrong? Somewhere along the line I seemed to have got all my values in life completely wrong. I had thought that to be a Christian was just a matter of attending Church fairly regularly, and although there was a great inner longing to attend more often than I did, in reality I didn't do much about satisfying that inner longing. I had barely scratched the surface in trying to understand what the name Christian implied or what it really meant in terms of discipleship and commitment.

I had felt, like lots of other young people of my time, that I had not much to offer and was afraid of being left on the shelf. As a result I had married a young man who, if I'm being honest, I spent more time rowing with than anything else, both before and after marriage. I should have seen the warning signs but I was at one and the same time naïve, young, and stupid. I was more interested in having a young man on my arm, a ring on my finger, a home of my own, and all that goes with it, and the freedom to do as I liked. I guess this need had arisen from spending several years in a children's home due to my mother's illness and, very sadly, her inability to look after me as a result of her ill-health. There was perhaps a need to feel secure. The importance of the step I was taking, and of being equally yoked in the sight of the Lord, didn't seem to filter through into that grey matter called a brain, despite the attempts made by the 'talk before the marriage ceremony' given by the Methodist Minister.

Looking back there were several warnings about the step I was taking. There was a certain and very grave disapproval from my mother's cousin and her husband, Auntie Lena and Uncle Victor, God-parents I loved dearly and who were extremely kind towards me and my parents. Were they taking their God-parent role very seriously? Probably so, although I didn't realise it at the time. There was even that minister's pre-marriage talk which, looking back, seemed to hold certain warnings and a somewhat unusual reservation which I hadn't quite perceived at that time. Oh for the gift of hindsight! And then there was the refusal from Uncle Victor, that beloved Godfather, to give me away at my wedding in place of my father, who was too ill to do so owing to a stroke which took away his speech. So my Mother's brother, Uncle Frank, graciously stepped in to do the honours.

Within a few years of marriage we started to go up in the world. We moved from an old semi-detached house with dreadful neighbours who liked to have parties and fool around with each other's partners (not something I approved of or took part in, I hasten to add). I dreaded the next invitation to a party and was continually thinking of excuses to get out of attending, and to persuade my husband of good reasons why we shouldn't attend. So it was a relief to move to the new house in another village several miles away. The house was a new Scandinavian design detached house on a new housing estate on the edge of lovely countryside. There was all that goes with the new 'image' – the fitted carpets, new furniture, and of course, better and eventually newer cars.

Eventually we became involved in local village organisations, gaining places on Committees and gradually rising to better and higher positions. The crème de la crème was when we were both elected to the local Town Council and became popular and much-loved figures in our neighbourhood. In the midst of this, deep down inside I knew something was not right. I had a good home, lovely friends, position in the community and a husband who by then had made a good career for himself and brought home a good wage. Why then was I so unhappy? Why was I not content with all these wonderful things and this good life?

I was almost too afraid to admit to myself but there was no escaping the fact that I had got my values in life very wrong. These things were not what made for happiness, and I was not at peace with myself or with God. I had also realised not long into the marriage that this had not been a right choice, but by the time I realised this it was far too late to do anything about it. I had either been very naïve or just too stubborn to heed those warning signs given by my parents and by other kindly relatives who wanted what was best for me. But like most young people in every age the more they tried to warn me the more I saw it as interfering, and the more stubborn and immovable I became. Looking back one realises the reality of the saying 'one cannot put an old head on young shoulders'. We do indeed get older and wiser, but by then the harm has often been done and it's too late to reverse it.

Over a period of time things went from bad to worse as both my husband and I became unsettled with our life-style. This was not helped by two holidays in Canada to see my long-lost relations, the good life-style over there, the friendliness of the people, the cultural diversity living happily side by side, and my deep longing to be near these loving relations whom I had only recently got to know and love. After a series of disasters – during which we had tried unsuccessfully to emigrate to Canada, and when I had been stranded in Canada as I had gone out there and tried to sort out what was happening with immigration – there came the inevitable marriage break-up. The circumstances leading up to it and the divorce process, must remain hidden. Things happened at that time which I will never understand, which I believe I am not meant to, and which I believe are not for divulging as they could be hurtful to others.

However I feel it is right to issue some notes of warning to the reader here. Warning number one is about not allowing ourselves to be ruled by worldly values. It is only natural to want a home and nice things around one and there is nothing wrong in that. But if we allow ourselves and our money, time, and energy to completely take us over in this way then we may end up on a very slippery downward slope.

The second is a warning from the Bible, and in connection with those matters which I feel I cannot discuss surrounding the time of the marriage break-up. There is a danger of becoming embroiled in things of the spirit-world which we do not understand and which are very dangerous. We hear much about people being caught up in religious cults and being taken away from home and loved ones, and although it was not that way with me, and I certainly didn't join a cult or worship other spirits, nevertheless something did happen to me which I didn't then and may never understand. These other-worldly and often evil influences may come to us in many varied guises as Satan is a Master at counterfeit, and they may offer all kinds of rewards or kicks, but we need always to examine them carefully and recognise them for what they are. The Bible warns us not to get involved with spirits or the spirit-world, and some of these evils are very subtle in their approach to us for Satan is a great deceiver. We only have to think about those things which Satan offered to Jesus during His forty days in the wilderness to realise how he is continually at work to deceive and to detract from the purposes of God. As a Christian I now know that it needs a great deal of soul-searching and guidance from wiser Christians to avert such dangers. Believe me, if one gets on that kind of roller-coaster, however plausible the ideal or the person may seem, it can destroy one's life. I can remember a time in my life when I felt that the only way out was to commit suicide. Thank God I was too cowardly for that. Be assured that nothing which brings true happiness and fulfilment in this life would ever bring us to the point of contemplating suicide. While I was in Canada, Irene, back home in England, had a great sense that I was in moral danger and set up a circle of people to pray earnestly for me (she told me this when I returned from Canada and went to live with her and Joe). These prayers availed much and it was some of these praying people who were to play an important part in my coming to Christ.

The Bible reminds us 'God **so loved** the world that He gave His only begotten Son, that whosoever believeth in Him should have everlasting life' (John 3:16). If ever we get to the point of deep despair we need to remember and read those words over and over again. There is only one source of true happiness, only one way, and that is Jesus Christ who came to bring us life in all its fullness. We only have to read the latter part of the Book of James, Chapter 3, to see what he had to say on this very subject. 'But the wisdom from above is pure first of all; it is also peaceful, gentle, and friendly; it is full of compassion and produces a harvest of good deeds; it is free from prejudice and hypocrisy'. If we become embroiled in anything which does not conform to those gentle and high-principled virtues, then it is not of the Spirit of God and we must turn from it as quickly as possible. This verse from the Bible is a very good guide to follow if we are trying to discern what is good and right.

So... although I had made a fresh start after divorcing my husband, I had a great awareness of sin, of my own part in all the failure of the broken marriage and of my life. Whatever the Law said about whose fault it really was, and about the actual reality of the situation, I still felt dreadful. I felt I should have tried to get it right from the very beginning or, looking at it realistically, shouldn't have even been there. I should have known better. I should have avoided making the mistakes in the first place and wanting a 'quick-fix' in so many areas of my life.

So here, in this lovely village on the outskirts of Leeds, with these loving Christians, I desperately wanted to make this fresh start and to follow the way of Jesus, but how could I forget all that had gone before? I did not have that strength of character. How foolish I was to think that I alone could do this thing, to think that I, Virginia, could effect the change in me. It was not I who was to make all things new, but God, the great I AM, with whom all things are possible. Only by His grace can each of us be made new.

From that Spring of 1981, and for quite some time to come, I was to learn much of this 'grace of God', beautifully described somewhere as 'the love of the loveliest falling on the unlovable and making it lovely'. I had committed my life to Christ and sincerely sought to follow Him and to be that new person – yet at times I was so weighed down with the past that it was almost as if I was drowning in guilt, self-pity, and recriminations. People were still loving and kind, helping me to put my life together, and accepting me regardless of what had gone before. During this time however, I did have to cope with the few Christians who, though loving towards me, did not agree with separation or divorce and I found that most hurtful. Sadly, due to the very nature of what had gone on in my marriage, the details of which I felt were not for telling, they would never know or understand them. This made for lack of the understanding and acceptance I needed from some of them. At times it was hard to bear. I urge the reader to think very carefully before condemning such persons. It is very easy to 'put on a face' for the outside world when in fact one's private and unseen life is desperately falling apart in ways completely unseen or unknown by even those who are closest. There are things which happen in a person's private life which some would find hard to believe if they were aware of them. Despite all of this in my life there was still this terrible guilt, until...

CHAPTER THREE

A NEW LIFE

**"Behold I am doing a new thing;
it is happening already'**

(Isaiah 43 : 19)

...UNTIL THE DAY I met Jesus; until the day I had a personal encounter with Him – a personal encounter as opposed to seeing Him through the love of others. The day and the details are so vivid that they are imprinted on my mind forever. It was an autumn evening in 1982, a really beautiful evening with blue sky and sunshine. Two very kind friends had asked me to go along with them to a service at St Matthias's Church on the outskirts of Leeds. I had heard quite a lot about this Anglican Church in recent months. It sounded very different to the staid Anglican services of my upbringing, the Anglican Church which I had left for the Methodist Church. My friends spoke of singing choruses, laying on of hands for healing, and of speaking in tongues. I was a little wary of their invitation, unsure and, if I'm being honest, a little afraid, not quite knowing what to expect. But my friends were fairly insistent and having invited me a few times already – and having promised them I *would* go one day – I didn't like to say "no" yet again. Anyway, what on earth was there to be afraid of? I was going with very deeply spiritual friends to a church service. I had no idea why it bothered me so much. I suspect it boiled down to a simple fear of the unknown, coupled with Satan's determined attempts to frustrate God's purpose for that evening. Looking back I can indeed see that was the reason. But God's purpose was not to be frustrated and I decided I would indeed go with them. Little did I know until later that both of my friends, husband and wife Paul and June, had individually felt 'led' to take me along with them that particular evening; it had not been a joint decision.

The Service was beautiful, reverently beautiful. And yet I still sat there feeling very afraid and with my heart pounding madly for no known or logical reason. There was singing of choruses (modern worship songs) followed by the most beautiful singing in tongues. I had never experienced this before and it was like nothing I had ever heard, like an angelic choir. I have heard singing in tongues many times since and it never fails to move me deeply. Throughout it all the faces in the congregation were glowing, lit up with joy as together they praised and worshipped God. Then an old man with snowy white hair and a gentle kindly voice, preached a sermon – a wonderfully comforting and uplifting sermon. I felt comforted by his message but **still** afraid.

"Shall we have a time of quiet prayer as we listen to what God is saying – I feel sure He has a message for someone here tonight" he said. At this, the curate's bidding, a deep hush settled on the congregation as we sat there in silent prayer.

Silence...this lasted for what seemed an age and then, from the quietness and peace of that packed and large congregation, came one voice. It was a man's voice and he was speaking in a language I had heard only once before when, kneeling together in prayer with Irene, she had spoken in tongues – my first experience of this gift of the Spirit. The language this time was either Hebrew or Aramaic. Silence again. Then came another voice, strong and full of authority, yet at the same time with a kind and loving intonation. This time the speech was English, and as he started to speak it was as if someone had suddenly switched a light on; I suddenly understood what St Paul was writing about in his letter to the Church at Corinth, when he told them how to conduct themselves when speaking in tongues and when there was interpretation of those tongues. The language of Jesus was Aramaic, and now this man was giving us, by the activity of the Holy Spirit in him, an English interpretation of what God had said in Aramaic through the first person.

"Do not be afraid; you are My child. I love you and I want to help you". My heart leaped for joy; instant recognition; it was my Lord, and I **knew** that He was speaking to me. Me! It was not unlike the meeting between Mary the Mother of Jesus and Elizabeth, in Luke Chapter 1, when the child in Elizabeth's womb recognized the child in Mary's womb and leaped for joy – instant recognition. Suddenly I was flooded by an immense inner peace and a sense of complete calm. The fear which had possessed me all evening left me instantly, and my heart stopped pounding madly as it had been doing till that moment. And then the second voice came again...

"...do you not know that you are My dear child"? Did I not know? How could I stupidly have ever doubted this fact? After all, we are told in the Bible, Romans Chapter 8, 'For the Spirit that God gives you does not make you slaves and cause you to be afraid; instead the Spirit makes you God's children, and by the Spirit's power we cry out to God, "Father! My Father!" God's Spirit joins Himself to our spirits to declare that we are God's children'.

It is amazing how one suddenly becomes aware of some great truth. In that moment of time, very suddenly, I comprehended the very great and very individual love that God has for each one of us. I realised suddenly what people meant when they talked of a personal Saviour; One who cared deeply about each individual; One who puts so much worth on each one of us that He died on the cross for me. In the words of that great man Charles Wesley, when writing of his conversion experience... .'He had taken away my sins, **even mine**.' He loved me so much that He had died for me, even me; the one who had strayed away from Him, rejected Him and His Church, yoked myself unequally in marriage, and then broken those marriage vows.

The voice was still speaking, interpreting the speech in tongues, and so much of what was uttered was so relevant to me, to my fears and problems and to the way I felt. Then throughout the whole congregation, as God gave His gifts through the Holy Spirit, there were many other confirmations of what had just been said. In his sermon the old man had talked of 'taking off the old and putting on the new', signifying the casting off of the old life and living in the newness of life with Jesus, and as I listened to these other voices of confirmation, the one spoken phrase which came over most forcibly to me were the words 'forget the ties of the past'.

First the words of reassurance, then of love, then the direction to forget the past, to go forward into a new life. From that point in time I never looked back. I knew what it was to feel release from past sins and failures; to be forgiven; to be given the chance to wipe the slate completely clean and to start afresh. The prophet Isaiah said 'He has sent me to proclaim liberty to the captives' and I knew that Jesus came to do that for each one of us – to free us from the sins and the fear which bound us captive. He had done that on the cross of Calvary for me, and again that night.

It is important to realise that when the Holy Spirit comes in this way He works in very different ways. The message given is for the edification of the whole church. This means that whilst I knew for a certainty that the message was personal for me there were almost certainly others in the congregation for whom it was also important. The words of the sermon would mean different things to different people, as would the activity of the Holy Spirit working through the gift of tongues and interpretation of those tongues. Just as what happened to me that night was very special so there would be many others there for whom it was special also, as the Holy Spirit spoke to many needs.

I walked out of the Church with my friends and into the evening sunlight. The experience was like walking from a dark prison into the bright light of the outside world with all its promise of hope for the future. I can remember vividly standing outside that Church, chatting to my friends, and feeling free – so free! 'My chains fell off, my heart was free; I rose, went forth, and followed Thee'. I can never sing the words of that hymn now without remembering how I felt that evening. I had met with Jesus, and I was 'free'.

CHAPTER FOUR

ADVENTURES IN GUIDANCE

'We are assured and know that, God being a partner in their labour, all things work together and are fitting into a plan for good to and for those who love God and are called according to His design and purpose

(Romans 8 : 28 Amp)

"I'M SURE THE Lord is telling you just to wait and to trust, Ginny". Auntie Irene (as I referred to her in those early days) was such a spiritually wise lady and her words made sense. She walked so close to her Lord and always seemed to know exactly what to do, and when. We had knelt together at the bedside that morning and prayed that the Lord would show me the way forward, and Irene had spoken in tongues as we had knelt there. It was after this 'happening' that she said these words, and although I didn't yet understand this 'praying in tongues' I felt sure she was right and had much confidence in her advice. If only I had some vague idea of what I ought to be doing. I had now reached the point where I needed to make a proper life for myself again – to find a job, some kind of home, and some measure of independence. But where could I start? That very day I had walked miles into the countryside to make enquiries about a caravan site where I had been led to understand I

Virginia and Irene

could site a caravan permanently. Perhaps not a very exciting prospect but at least it would have been a home of sorts, and a start. I was willing to try anything. Unfortunately the caravan idea came to nothing.

My finances were rather limited owing to the fact that as a Christian I felt it inappropriate to ruin my former husband's life by making maintenance claims on him. Whatever the wrongs of the past, he too had his life to live and a fresh start to make, and I did not want him to feel that I was a continual shadow in the background of his life, continually draining any resources he might have. I guess, looking back, that this was a kind of forgiveness, although in later life I realised that this attitude had lost me any pension claim I may have had on him and I did often wonder whether I had indeed done the right thing. I have comforted myself since with the thought that at that time I had taken that decision for what I believed were right and honourable reasons. But the J.P at the divorce hearing had been so hard on me for not making that claim. My embarrassment was further compounded by the fact that the the he was a Methodist Local Preacher and a member in the same Church as I was now attending! But sometimes we learn too late and all we can do is console ourselves with that thought that what we did came from right and honourable motives, however misguided they may turn out to be.

The residue from the sale of our joint home after payment of what was owed to the Building Society was meagre and I had used most of my share – rightly or wrongly – to pay off to other parties what I felt were debts of honour and which my former husband refused to pay. Whether in fact they had been necessary I also now query but at the time I had again done what I felt was right. I suppose that this was part and parcel of the changed attitudes which came about through becoming a Christian and perceiving different things as important or otherwise. Also the upbringing I had received from my parents had a bearing on this as well. My Father was always instilling in me such things as 'tell the truth and shame the devil' etc. Things like that tend to stick down the years and shape a kind of moral code.

So what on earth was I to do for a job? I needed to stop being a burden on Auntie Irene and Uncle Joe, the loving couple who had taken me in, and begin to pay my way. Most of my working life till that point had been spent doing office work in all kinds of different employments, apart from a seven year stint when I had done quite a bit of taxi-driving for a family concern run by a very kindly Christian couple. I had worked in two worsted mill offices, one as general office assistant, and the other as trainee wages clerk. I had worked in a TV rental company shop as cashier, taking rental payments from customers. Another job I had worked in a small electrical contractors company, running the office for them. Others had included a stint in a large Drapers Store as an assistant in the Millinery Department; a short stint in a residential children's nursery, where I had hoped to train for work with young children. The latter came to nought as I left very quickly when I found that the staff were visited often by soldiers from a nearby army camp, and I didn't like the things which went on between them. I had also spent some time serving in a confectioners shop – the job being obtained for me by my mother who was a friend of the family. So although I was quite good at dealing with money, typing, etc, I had absolutely no qualifications because I had missed a great deal of schooling as a child due to ill-health. I had a smattering of practical experience at all kinds of things. I was 38 years old and at that time even school-leavers and highly qualified people coming out of University couldn't find work – what chance had I?

Secretly I hoped that I might find further driving work. The taxi-driving experience had been marvellous and as one who was basically shy I had really enjoyed the one to one interaction with the customers as this had brought me out of my shell. There had, of course, always been the difficulty of keeping to the speed limit set by Law whilst trying to get people to railway stations or airports! I had loved working for this couple in their family firm. They were most kind to me and to all who worked for them and were more like friends than employers. Looking back the contact with them was just one of a string of contacts throughout my life with very kindly Christian people, and I am sure they had been part of God's plan. But back to the work problem. I adored office work, and enjoyed writing letters, but my typing was only self-taught and rather slow, and the shorthand I had done at night school had been an absolute nightmare and a complete non-starter. I did have secret hopes that my fondness for small children (a love inherited from my Mother who had held several jobs caring for children) might bring in work for baby-sitting or Mother's help work.

I had come to the point where I must find work as there wasn't much money left in the kitty. I loved Irene and Joe like a daughter by now but they needed their privacy, and their spare room back for their family and friends, and more importantly I needed to pay my way. Little did I know how wonderfully God was to take care of all my needs.

So down to practicalities. First to 'sign on' at the Department of Employment. That was an eye-opener. Down and out as I felt at that time I found that there were lots of people far worse off than me. With the inevitable waiting around one cannot help becoming involved in the lives of others who are also 'waiting around'.

I got into conversation with a lady who had been sleeping rough and hadn't even got the money for her bus fare to a place where she could secure a bed for the night. Hers was a sad tale of woe, of being pushed from pillar to post, and I wondered how many others there were with similar stories to tell.

It was interesting, if not disturbing at times, to watch people come and go. Lots of them were young and wearing clothing which looked as if it had been handed down once, twice, or even three times. They might, of course, have come from second-hand or charity shops, assuming they could even afford that. Their faces were mostly drawn, weighed down by the cares of the world and by their inability to find work or to make ends meet. Eyes are often thought of as the mirror of the soul. For the most part these folk had dull, lifeless eyes which expressed a hopelessness of the soul.

In contrast to them I was lucky. I was dealt with by people who were courteous and helpful, and my assumption that I would not be allowed any kind of unemployment benefit proved false, which amazed me. However I arrived 'home' to Irene and Joe's that day feeling saddened by what I had seen, but very much counting my own blessings, and being conscious of God's care for me in numerous everyday ways.

A few weeks went by but despite signing on there was nothing in the post or the local newspapers to indicate any suitable work for me. Things were getting desperate and I had to think of something else rather than rely on the Department of Employment. I decided to put postcards in all the local shop windows, advertising my availability for work and telling of the few skills I possessed. For someone with very limited finances this worked out quite well as the charge for advertising in this way was only about 5-10p per week. The advert ran something like this:-

> 'Lady, 38 years old, requires work. Absolutely anything considered. Fond of children. Reasonable typist. Enjoys driving. Willing to do housework'.

The response was very slow at first, just one reply offering me a cleaning job for one morning a week. But it was a start and the lady who offered me the job was not a well person and desperately needed someone to help her. The bonus was her gorgeous little daughter, Jennifer, a delightful 2 year old with a cherub face, blond hair, and dimples when she smiled. Jennifer followed me around the house as I dusted and vacuumed, and it was an absolute delight to be in her presence.

I continued to knock on all the available doors of opportunity where work was concerned. Whilst doing so Irene, Joe and I continued to pray for God to open up His way for me. I was learning to want God's way for me more than anything else, and to trust Him to show me that way.

About a month later things really began to happen. I arrived 'home' from my half-day cleaning job and as soon as I got into the house the telephone started to ring. That afternoon was one of the most amazing and incredible days of my life. If I had been able to stand aside and watch it all it would have been like watching an expert on jigsaws very quickly and accurately put all the pieces together to make the perfect picture. But this was the work of The Expert, the Creator of the world, so I shouldn't have been surprised!

By teatime I had received **exactly** enough phone calls and offers of work – no more no less – to make exactly a 5-day working week. The majority of them were from individuals who wanted me to work just half a day each week, cleaning. One other call was from a lady who wanted someone for a few days a week, to look after her little 3 year old boy and also act as housekeeper.

Cleaning! My pride took a quick plunge. Although I loved driving and office work I had held secret hopes that the advert might have brought more in the care of children, and not any housework at all! Then just as quickly I had to shake myself and forget that thought as I realised how lucky I was to have any work at all, and my mind flashed back for an instant to the people I had talked to and seen in the Department of Employment.

Then I learnt from one of the ladies who offered me work that she had been praying about her cleaning problem and the matter of who she should employ. She was about my age and a glowing Christian. It appeared that I was her answer to prayer, and suddenly cleaning took on a very special role as I realised that the Lord considered me suitable for this task. She and her family became a great blessing to me as they befriended me, as we shared Christian fellowship together, and as they took me away on holiday to Cornwall with them and their two boys. I began to see that the Master's Hand had been at work, fitting all those pieces together perfectly.

CHAPTER FIVE

WAITING ON GOD

'My God will liberally supply, fill to the full, your every need. . .

(Philippians 4 : 19 Amp)

THE MASTER HAND at work, fitting together the pieces of my life. This was a process which noticeably started at that point but which I now know will go on throughout my earthly life, and had probably been happening long before this, although I was unaware of it. And this was just the very exciting beginning! If I could have known what joys in guidance and provision the Lord had in store for me I would not have been able to contain myself.

> How gracious is the Lord, our God,
> How infinite His ways,
> How small we feel when we survey

The wonders He displays;
And yet I know that it is true
He lived and died for me,
With awe I view His nail pierced hands
And cry 'How can it be'?
And yet I know that it is true,
For us, His cross He bore,
And we, in awe, can only kneel
And cry "Lord, we Thee, adore!"

(Irene – my mother in Christ)

I was extremely happy being 'self-employed' in all these different cleaning jobs. Without exception all the people I worked for were most kind, and amongst the slog of cleaning there were so many blessings. One of the couples I worked for found out that I enjoyed gardening and when the weather was nice, and the housework completed, I would be invited to go out and mow the lawns or weed the borders – I loved that! The area I was working in was exceptionally beautiful, the village of Bramhope on the outskirts of Leeds, and it was a delight and a privilege to be allowed to tend this lovely garden.

Another person I worked for occasionally allowed me to use her mini car to go home in, saving me the long treks up hill and down dale on my bicycle. I had purchased the latter on my meagre savings for getting to work and to save money on bus fares. This job, although hard work, was a particular delight as I looked after her little boy, Tristan, quite a lot. When the cleaning was done I would sometimes be asked to take him for a walk in the countryside, or at other times be allowed to drive this employer's very large Rover car to the Supermarket for her, taking Tristan with me.

After a little while I managed to find a tiny bed-sit in a village near my work places, and moved out from Irene and Joe's, able to give them the space they needed for themselves and their family and friends. I found that the salary from these various jobs was just enough to cover my rent, electric slot meter, food bill, and a tiny little bit to spare. And yet again God's provision for me through kind Christian friends was overwhelming as they helped me to find the bits and pieces of furniture and crockery that I needed for my bed-sit. Although things were not moving as quickly as I perhaps would have liked, I was beginning to learn to 'wait on God' and to trust Him for all my needs. In return He demonstrated to me His complete adequacy to supply those needs.

This was to be demonstrated to me in a greater way before too long. After a while the cleaning jobs began to take their toll on my health and Irene suggested that perhaps it was time to look for some other kind of work. There was again the dilemma about what on earth I could do. I started to study the newspapers regularly and eventually three jobs stood out, and I applied for them all at the same time. One was to work in a newly formed department of a hospital, helping provide aids for people with disabilities. The second was to be Warden of a Jewish Housing Association's Sheltered Housing Scheme. The third was that of Assistant Housekeeper at a Methodist Guild Holiday Hotel in Derbyshire. This last one Irene was very keen for me to apply for. I knew nothing of Methodist Guild Holidays but Irene and Joe had been to several of them on holiday, and they spoke highly of this Christian Organisation. So of the three this was the one I wanted most, the aids department came a close second, and the least attractive was the Warden job with the Jewish Housing Association – the latter not for any race or religious prejudice, I hasten to add! It was purely a matter of what kind of work did or didn't appeal.

How often life turns out so differently to what we expect. The interview in Derbyshire was very good and the place was in the most beautiful surroundings. However it became apparent very quickly during the interview that I did not have the skills needed for the task of assistant housekeeper, and although bitterly disappointed I had to accept this was not meant to be. I never got an interview for the hospital job and again, although disappointed, knew that my future was surely in God's hands. I did, however, get an interview for the job of Warden with the Jewish people. Surprisingly they didn't really expect me to have any First Aid training, or nursing experience, or qualifications of any kind. But what seemed important to them was a working knowledge of basic information which old people may need such as how to obtain benefits, who to contact about these, etc.

Interestingly in the past I had been involved in politics and the party I belonged to held occasional 'Welfare Benefits days' when we parked in an open-top wagon in the middle of a town or village and handed out benefits leaflets for people to read. As a Town Councillor I was also involved in a Surgery, helping people who came along with all kinds of problems, and so I had learnt where to go to obtain help for people. In this job before me it seemed that this knowledge would now be relevant. Whilst this was the job I had wanted least of all, it was the one I was offered and which I accepted, and again God was teaching me that all of the things we learn in life He can use for His purposes.

The other thing which came out at the interview was that they needed someone who was willing to work on a Saturday because this was the Sabbath day when Jewish people must not work. It seemed that in this respect Christians were most acceptable and this was fine by me. And so started the next phase of my life, and my walk with Jesus.

CHAPTER SIX

SERVICE FOR CHRIST

'. . . first for the Jew. . .' (Romans 1 : 16)

THE FIRST DAY of my new job dawned and it was with a certain amount of trepidation that I moved in my meagre belongings. No-one had told me that my first day there would not be a hectic round of getting to know people and understanding my work with them. Nor was I told that it was one of the most important days of the Jewish Year – The Day of Atonement – nor that this was a new Sheltered Housing development where no-one yet lived and that it would be a few days or weeks before everyone had moved in! So no-one was around on that first day, except...

... a horde of workmen, all having completed their work on this development and vying with each other to explain all kinds of systems to me so that they could leave and go on to their next job! There was the plumber who was anxious to tell me all about the plumbing and the central heating systems – where valves and stopcocks were; how the central heating system worked; how to set the time clocks; and how to bleed the radiators. Then there was the company who had put in the intercom system connected from my flat to all the others in the complex. Much explanation ensued about how that worked. Then there was.... STOP! By this time I had a complete mental block and was beginning to panic. Had I really been led into this work? Had I got it wrong? How on earth was I going to cope?

The workmen drifted away, all wrongly assuming that I had adequately taken in the mountain of instructions they had given me, and presumably not noticing how my eyes had glazed over! Quiet descended on this, as yet, unoccupied development of approximately 36 flats and bungalows. And in the quietness I began to question why I was here. As I realised the immensity of the work before me and the fact that it was all down to me, panic took hold of me with its very strongest grip. There was a knot in my stomach, and my mouth was as dry as a desert in the hottest season.

Before I could think any further there was a ring at the doorbell. Now what? Oh **please** God, not more instructions. I rushed down the stairs to my front door and flung it open with a certain amount of trepidation. In front of me stood a tall man and before I had time to ask who he was he said " Hello, I'm Paul. I'm from the local Methodist Church, and I've come to welcome you". What a relief – not another workman. I invited Paul in and he hardly had chance to sit down before I was pouring out to this complete stranger my concerns at this great task before me. Without further ado he started to pray about them. He prayed about the radiators, and the intercom system, and every little thing that troubled me, and what a sense of relief flooded over me as together we handed these things over to the care of God. When he had finished praying and we talked some more I was again assured that I was in the place God wanted me to be at this time, and that He would guide me as I went along. Little did I know at that time that Paul, his wife June, and their two children would become real firm friends for many years to come, and that they would be involved in many important aspects of my future life.

Before the residents started to move in, the Lord, through His people, provided much that was needed to furnish my lovely one bedroom flat that came with the job. Irene and Joe gave me a carpet they had in store, to use in my living room. A friend of the two doctors I had previously cleaned for, and who just happened to live along the road from my new abode, gave me four dining chairs. Someone else provided me with a Dining Table. Eventually I had all that I needed – all provided by people who belonged to Christ. Yet further confirmation that, daunting as the task in front of me seemed to be, I was in the right place and He had provided for my basic needs.

Little by little the residents moved in. It was an interesting time and, as they moved in bit by bit instead of all together in one fell swoop, there was time to get to know them. This was Sheltered Housing and for all of them was a great change to their lives. To an extent they had given up their independence by moving to where they would have a Warden always at hand in case they were ill or needed help to live as independently as possible. Some had given up lovely big homes and had sold furniture and possessions in order to fit into a smaller property, so it was quite a traumatic time for them.

The complex was a mixture of flats and bungalows set around a courtyard, with grassed areas and seating. There was no indoor communal lounge on this site (although one across the road on another site) so they all still had their own homes and could live quite independently from each other. Each dwelling had a living room, kitchen, bathroom, and one or two bedrooms. If ever they were unable to cope with making their own meals it was my responsibility to arrange for Meals on Wheels. I also had the role of making contact with them each morning to see they were okay, also being available via the intercom in my flat so they could call me at any time of day or night with a problem or emergency of any kind. A Social Worker from the Leeds Jewish Housing Association called at regular intervals, giving the opportunity to talk through residents problems or for me to express my concerns about any of them or about my own role. Once the scheme was up and running I was 'sold' on this way of living for older people who didn't want to entirely give up their independence, and even to this day I would recommend it to anyone in that position.

It was nice to get to know them all, and have the privilege of being their confidante in all kinds of matters. The fact that I was a Christian and, by this time a Local Preacher 'on note' and then 'on trial', did not seem to bother them at all. In fact, strange as it may seem, one or two of them took a really keen interest in my preaching studies and exams and were always asking me how I was going on! This despite the fact that I never strayed from the promise extracted from me by my employers at the interview not to evangelise them. I never sought to do so, but despite this they showed an interest in what I was doing and I answered them honestly without any need to "evangelise." God spoke to them in ways which were not of my making, and He knew what He was doing with me in that place. On the occasional Sundays when I had a preaching appointment many of them would tell me to make contact via the intercom system earlier than usual 'so you can catch your bus to get to Church on time, dear'.

It was hard work, especially when there were a lot of interruptions from the intercom during the night. One lady in particular, who had difficulty walking, got to a point where every time she had to visit the bathroom in the night she would fall and be unable to get up. Night after night the intercom would go, or the man who lived above her would hear her cries and call me. I would rush round to see if she was okay, and there were frequent calls to the ambulance service who would come out and lift her up so I could help her back to bed. She was a very large and heavy lady so there was no way I could lift her on my own. This happened the night before one of my Local Preaching exams and as I sat at the desk the following day, trying to take in the questions I was supposed to answer in an essay, I felt like a zombie – I was so tired. Amazingly I passed the exam, and never quite knew how.

The pay was very poor, but my needs were met via a rent-free flat, unlimited free use of the telephone in the flat, and other fringe 'benefits in kind' such as free electricity, etc. However when it got to the end of the month I very often almost ran out of money to buy food. That was until Soli (Solomon) moved in. Soli was a very active man and took great delight in helping the other residents. He would go to the shops for them and sometimes even offered to do my shopping as well, besides other little kindnesses. He had no idea how small my pay was, nor that I struggled for money to provide for my meals just before pay-day each month. However not long after he moved in he would ring the doorbell on a very regular basis and tell me he had just made a casserole dish and had made far more than he could eat. "Would you take some of this meal off me" he would say, "I've made far more than I can possibly eat." This always happened at the point in the month where I didn't know where my next meal was coming from and Soli had no idea of that. Coincidence? I believe not, and I am convinced that God works through all kinds of people to provide for our needs. When this happened I was reminded that it was through the most unexpected source that the Israelites were freed from bondage in Egypt and allowed to go back to their homeland, and it was through the most unexpected man – Cyrus – whom God had chosen to work His will at that time. Soli was my Cyrus, the most unexpected person, chosen by God to make sure my needs were met.

During the two years I was there I particularly enjoyed the summer months when residents sat out on the seats in the courtyard around which their homes were set. I used to sit with them and once they knew I had a guitar they encouraged me to play to them. I couldn't play well but managed to strum several tunes we all knew and we would have most congenial times of singing along together. I felt very much like Maria from 'The Sound of Music' except that I had a group of elderly people around me rather than a group of children!

Eventually the lack of proper cover for days off and increasing nightly interruptions began to take their toll on my health and Irene (now very much my Mother in Christ, and referring to herself as 'Mum') felt it was time for me to look for other work. So again that same question arose in my mind 'what on earth can I do'? I now had two years of experience as a Sheltered Housing Warden under my belt, but was that enough? By now I had learnt to pray about every aspect of my life, so I committed this to the Lord and started to look for other work, to 'knock on the doors' as we Christians call it. By praying and then actively seeking God's will there was no way that He would allow me to go astray from it. There seemed very little that was suited to my capabilities, except what appeared to be a lovely job as a Warden in a Christian Sheltered Housing complex on the outskirts of London. I applied and to my great delight received an interview. I struggled my way down to London on the train; then followed instructions about which tube to catch. The latter was a nightmare as the escalators in parts of the Underground are extremely long and high, and with my morbid fear of heights I found this not only daunting but very frightening. I eventually found the place, had an interview with a lovely bunch of people, and felt I had a very good chance of getting the job. I felt I could be very happy there. It was with great dismay that shortly afterwards I received a letter telling me I had not been successful but that I was second on the list and if anything went wrong with the preferred applicant I would be contacted again.

From then on there seemed no openings at all, and I was becoming more and more despondent. My lady relief cover for my one day off during the week was playing up and not allowing me time off, and nightly interruptions were becoming more and more frequent. Every time the intercom buzzer went off during the night I suffered dreadful palpitations as I awoke suddenly. I was so exhausted that I wondered how much longer I could hold out. I loved the old people dearly, but my health was beginning to suffer and I knew that I must try and find something else.

Irene was such a comfort during this time, making sure that when I did manage my days off I spent them with her in her home on the other side of Leeds, where she cosseted and cared for me. The following was what she penned to me during one of my more difficult moments:

Oh Ginny dear, see here, see here,
The World's not at an end
Because you've got the Lord,...and me!
And many another friend.

But darling, oh I understand,
It's disappointing when
You've built up hopes and longing plans,
And they're destroyed by men,
In fact, they haven't got a clue
Of what you really need,
A nice companionable girl
To share in thought and deed
Who willingly would do her part
In buzzer, nights, and care,
And take a little of the load
And in the burden share.
You're tired and sadly need a rest,
A giggle and some fun,
You need to sleep quite undisturbed
Till all exhaustion's gone.
So Lord, of Ginny, please take care
She's precious Lord, to me,
I love her and she needs a rest,
Her happy self to be.
You know just what she needs dear Lord,
Please gently lift her load

And help her carry it along
This very stony road.
And send a little bit of light
A star to guide her way
And on the morrow give her strength
Sufficient for the day.
Lord, humbly do we come to Thee,
And say "Yes Lord, You know
Your plans are sure, Your love supreme,
And in Your steps we'll go".

(Irene – mother in Christ)

One day Irene suggested to me that if I was thinking of a holiday I ought to go on a Methodist Guild Holiday. A holiday? Surely she knew how little money I had? The very idea of a holiday seemed quite out of the question. To this day I cannot remember how on earth I afforded it. I do not recall anyone lending me or giving me any money, and have no idea how I managed to afford it – it remains a mystery hidden within the depths of my mind. I knew vaguely about the Methodist Guild, as during my time in Leeds I had attended some Guild meetings at a Methodist Church some distance away, and prior to that had been for that job interview at Willersley Castle in Derbyshire. That was two years ago, but I still knew relatively little about their holidays.

I managed to book a place at one of their holiday centres in Cumbria, at Grange-over-Sands, but had no inkling that this was to be a life-changing experience in very many ways. Nor did I realise that the waiting I had to endure as regards a job was all about God's perfect timing. What joy He had in store for me.

CHAPTER SEVEN

PREPARATIONS

'...and then for the Gentiles' (Romans 1 : 16)

DURING MY WEEK at Abbott Hall at Grange-over-Sands I learnt quite a bit about Methodist Guild Holidays. They had their origins in the meeting known as The Wesley Guild, where people of all ages and both sexes came together for fellowship and fun. Eventually a group of them decided that it would be good to share on holiday the kind of fellowship and fun that was experienced on a weekly meeting basis. From these small beginnings grew the organisation known as Methodist Guild Holidays which, at the time I had my holiday, had nine centres throughout Britain. Those existing at that time were at Whitby, North Yorkshire; Grange-over-Sands, Lancashire; Cromford, Derbyshire; Colwyn Bay, North Wales; The Wye Valley on the Welsh Borders; Sidmouth, Devon; Eastbourne, Sussex; St Ives, Cornwall; and Swanage, Dorset.

What a joy it was to be at Abbot Hall. First there was the sheer bliss of being away from intercoms and calls in the middle of the night, and the opportunity to have a proper night's sleep. I hadn't realised how utterly exhausted I was until I went away and started to take life more gently. I then remembered Irene's prayer to the Lord for me, written in poetry form. It had certainly been answered.

All the folk there were Christians, from different backgrounds and denominations, and although I dearly loved my old Jewish folk it was nice to be amongst one's own people and to share Christian fellowship, conversation and fun with them. Until I went there I hadn't quite realised just how much I missed Christian fellowship and companionship. Although still quite introvert and shy I soon made friends, and one very loving older couple, Mary and Joseph, quickly took me under their wing and were so kind to me. Irene had urged me to take my guitar with me; she explained that guests were encouraged to entertain, and so I also soon made friends with the young folk on the holiday. So much further on in my life it is hard to remember the full details of that week except that every aspect of it was absolute sheer bliss. However two very distinct things will remain in my memory forever.

The first was the Social Secretary working at Abbott Hall. As we went with her on coach trips and walks and enjoyed the evening entertainment she arranged, I started to think to myself 'now that's a job I could do; I don't need A or O levels for this and all I have done in the past has been enough to give me the abilities that this job requires'. At that time there was no thought of God calling me to that kind of work, it just confirmed that there were jobs around which I could do and which didn't make the usual academic demands.

The other was an experience which was like a foretaste of heaven. One particular day we had a coach trip to the lovely little village of Hawkshead in the Lake District. As we alighted from the coach we all went in different directions – some to see the sights, some to look at the shops. As usual Mary, Joseph and I naturally gravitated together and we all agreed that we would go and see the little Methodist Chapel in the village. One of them had an inkling that there was an organ in there which visitors were allowed to play. Sure enough a notice in the Chapel said so. Mary could play and Joseph, who had a lovely voice, liked to sing, as I did. So Mary started to play hymns and Joseph and I sang. After a while we got completely caught up in singing praise to God, and time slipped away unnoticed. I was vaguely aware of people (tourists) coming into the Church and joining in the singing, some of them requesting certain hymns. Then they would slip away and others would come and go. The three of us became completely oblivious to the world around us. During this time I had a heightened awareness of the wonderful fellowship of those who joined us and then moved on, even though we hardly noticed or spoke to each other. When we finally came down from heaven to earth it was time to go back to the coach for our onward journey.

For me that was a very real foretaste of heaven. We know what the Bible tells us of heaven, but we do not really know what it will be like. That is for us to wait and find out. But we do know that we will rejoice together around the throne of God and of the Lamb, and I believe that when we do so although we might be aware of others around us our thoughts will essentially be centred on Him who sits on the throne. That experience in the Methodist Chapel at Hawkshead is the nearest I can imagine to what it will be like – a tremendous sense of the joy of worshipping God together with others, but above all being caught up in that worship to the point that one forgets oneself and thinks only of the worship and of Him who is the centre of it.

Back down to earth after the holiday I returned to the Sheltered Housing complex wondering how I would cope with the difficulties I had to face there. Awaiting me on my doormat was the 'Methodist Recorder'. Still longing for another job I walked up the stairs to my flat, dropped my luggage and, before doing anything else, turned to the 'Situations Vacant' pages. The advertisement stood out glaringly. 'Methodist Guild Holidays, Moorlands, Whitby, requires a full-time permanent Social Secretary'. Wow! The very job I had been watching someone do all week and thought 'I could do that' was vacant. And it was vacant in that wonderful north east coastal town of Whitby, a place I had loved from childhood. I knew without a second thought that I had to apply for it, and this was why nothing had come up for me before.

I rang up for an application form. The deadline date was only about two days away but I was told by the Manageress not to worry about the application or the date but to come along in the next few days and bring a reference. An appointment for an interview was made there and then, even though she didn't have a clue about who I was or what I had done in the past! I was a little worried about the need for a reference but as I read my daily Scripture readings a passage from 2 Corinthians chapter 3 stood out very clearly to me. It said this "...do we need, like some people, letters of recommendation...? You yourselves are our letter, written on our heart, known and read by everybody. You show that you are a letter from Christ, the result of our ministry, written not with ink but with the Spirit of the Living God, not on tablets of stone but on tablets of human hearts. Such confidence as this is ours through Christ before God. Not that we are competent in ourselves to claim anything for ourselves, but our competence comes from God'. Although not taking this passage completely in context I felt the Lord was telling me not to worry about my lack of a reference; He would be His own recommendation and make me competent for the task He was calling me to. I was to find both of these things completely true.

Then began the task of organising my travel to Whitby, and what a task that turned out to be! The replies from both the rail network and the bus companies ran along similar lines. "Sorry love but we don't go to Whitby in the winter months" (this was late October) and "it would be a lot easier if you just decided to go in summer". But I couldn't go in summer, the job was NOW. One company suggested that the only way I could get there was to drive, but I hadn't got a car. What on earth was I to do?

As it happened I had made a new friend recently. Chris (Christine) worked in the nearby National Children's Home, was a Christian, and a friend of Irene and Joe. And also quite by chance – or was it – we happened to talk on the phone just at this time, and I shared my problems. "I think I might be able to help, Ginny" she said, "just give me a little time and I'll ring you back". Not long after she phoned back and told me with glee that she could borrow a car and would take me there, "provided that I can bring Samuel along". Samuel was her gorgeous little boy, not yet at school, so she needed to be able to bring him.

So on a beautiful autumn day we all set out for Whitby. We followed the instructions and found the Methodist Guild Holiday Hotel – Moorlands – in a lovely position on the cliff top, overlooking the sea. Nervously I rang the doorbell and we were warmly welcomed in by a member of staff. Chris and Samuel were looked after and I was shown upstairs to the first floor office. "Hello, I'm Marjorie Brown" said a beaming faced lady with twinkling eyes and a warm smile, "come and sit down". I was far too early for the interview and the House Director who should be interviewing me had been held up, so Marjorie and I started talking. I noticed that she walked with sticks and that her hands were gnarled and twisted and she had those special shoes – obviously arthritis of some kind. Almost immediately Marjorie started to pour out about her need for a Social Secretary to work alongside her who understood her and her specific needs. Having worked with old people for over 2 years I had learnt the art of listening and so it wasn't difficult to just sit and listen to Marjorie and to sympathise with her special situation. I felt I had been prepared for this. This was only the first small glimpse of a wonderful lady who, despite her illness, did the most fantastic job of managing this place and endeared herself to those who got to know her well. As we talked my heart was warming to this lady and to the job I now hoped might be mine. But it was up to the House Director.

After what seemed an age of talking about all manner of things, through the door walked the House Director, Mr Eric Arundale. And so the interview began. Interview? It was certainly the most interesting and unusual interview I have ever had. There were none of the usual daunting questions which one wonders how to answer or whether one has answered correctly – passed the test, so to speak. It was more like a cosy chat with a good friend (Marjorie Brown) and a kindly uncle (Eric Arundale). In the years that followed I was to find that Mr Arundale was indeed an archetypal kindly uncle to all the staff at Moorlands – all of whom loved him and his wife immensely.

The chatting continued and time seemed to fly by. Then I suddenly heard Marjorie ask a question. "You do realise, don't you, that whatever the weather, even if it's pouring with rain, if the guests want a walk then you'll be expected to take them on a walk? How do you feel about that?" Did I really form the words I heard myself say? "Provided I can keep my hair dry I won't mind one bit" I said. No sooner had I uttered those words of vanity than I realised what I had said. Oh no! Had I blown my chances of this job? Marjorie and Mr Arundale roared with laughter. Then they asked me to leave the office for a few minutes whilst they chatted this through. I was shown downstairs and into the dining room where the table was being prepared for staff lunch. Christine, Samuel and I were invited to join them. I was amazed at their generosity. We had hardly started to eat when Marjorie and Mr Arundale came in the dining room and without more ado told me I had got the job and asked me how soon I could start!

I was amazed. The holiday at Abbott Hall flitted into my mind, and the picture of the lady doing the Social Secretary job, which I had suddenly felt was something I could easily do despite having no qualifications. I then knew for a certainty that this was all part of God's Plan and that this place, here in Whitby, was where I was meant to be. I cannot describe the joy which flooded through my heart at this certainty that I was soon to be here in the centre of God's will.

The meal continued, and lovely little Samuel entranced the staff throughout what was more like a large family gathering. I did not know it but this was to be the pattern of life at this place, and there were to be many more meal-times such as this, eaten alongside people who were to become like brothers and sisters to me.

The three of us spent the rest of the day exploring Whitby before we eventually left to return to Leeds. Although having to return to a job which had become over-burdensome to me, it was now with a heart lifted above the despair of the burdens, in the knowledge that I would soon be starting a new life in a new and beautiful place. Even more joyful was the fact that I would soon be working alongside those who were also Christians, and meeting up with many more who would come as guests.

The next few weeks were frenetic with some items to pack up and others to dispose of. I could not take furniture with me as I would no longer have a flat but just a small bedroom to live in. However the furniture and other saleable items went quickly, and provided just enough money for the essentials of my new life. I was sorry to leave the old people with whom I had become very close but I knew without a doubt that this was right to do. I remembered what someone had told me 'The Lord will never place on you a burden which is more than He will give you strength to cope with'. I had learnt the truth of that and also realised that sometimes the strength to cope is provided by those around us, and in this Sheltered Housing Scheme in Leeds that help had slowly dwindled away. It was time to move on and the Lord was now taking the burden away and replacing it with a job I could cope with. The old people were most kind and collected some money to provide me with a leaving gift. It could not have been more appropriate. It was a beautiful tan leather suitcase with my initials embossed in gold. I did not have a suitcase to my name and this allowed me to leave that place and arrive in Whitby with dignity.

It was here also that Michael was a blessing to me. I had known Michael when, in my late teens, I had changed my allegiance from the Anglican to the Methodist Church. There I had met Irene and Joe for the first time. They were both Local Preachers and also the leaders of the Youth Club in the Methodist Church I joined in Holmfirth, West Yorkshire. For those who don't know it, Holmfirth is that lovely place portrayed in the television series 'Last of the summer wine' and was my birthplace and my home for several years. Irene and Joe were wonderful Christians and all the young people adored them. They had three children, John, Ian and Patrick. And then there was Michael. Michael was their kind-of adopted son who lived with them. I say kind-of because he went to live with them when he lost his parents, and to all intents and purposes he became another son to them. We teenagers had done much together both in and out of the Church, and had all become quite close.

Since arriving in Leeds I had met up with Mike again, along with his wife Valerie, as they lived not very far from Irene and Joe. So the friendship had been rekindled, and Mike and Val had been very kind to me. Now Mike helped me with moving my small belongings to Whitby, taking some things over before my actual move. I was so fortunate to have such kind friends.

CHAPTER EIGHT

THE BEGINNING OF THE REST OF MY LIFE

'For I know the plans I have for you' declares the Lord, 'plans to prosper you and not to harm you, plans to give you a future and a hope' (Jeremiah 29 : 11)

SO THE DAY dawned. The day that was to welcome me to a new home, a new place of work, and to new friends whose numbers I could never have envisaged. Looking back I cannot remember how many multitudes of times my heart lifted as I travelled back from holidays at home spent with Irene in Huddersfield, and passed over that harbour bridge back into Whitby. Most people feel sad at going back to work after a break but since my day of arrival, Whitby has always had this effect on me. Each time I left, and then returned, I was happy to be back

I travelled to Whitby by train. Yes, a train did happen to run that day in November, despite what had been said at the time of my interview! The second part of the journey was from near Middlesbrough via the Esk Valley line to Whitby, the most beautiful track I have ever travelled on. The train went over little viaducts with wonderful views in the distance. There were woodlands and streams and waterfalls alongside the track – just beautiful. The day, despite being mid-November, was sunny and beautiful, and whilst being slightly nervous of this new venture, I had the most tremendous sense of peace in my heart. I cannot describe this peace, except to say I had never experienced such before, and it spoke to me of travelling to the place where God wanted me to be. It was indeed 'the peace that passes understanding.'

When the taxi from the Railway Station dropped me at the door of 'Moorlands' there was another slight twinge of nervousness but that was quickly dispelled by Brenda, one of the staff, as she flung the front door open wide, took my case off me and welcomed me in with a wide and friendly smile. I was shown up to my room – a tiny room at the front of the house with a wonderful view out to sea. Fantastic! All of my life I will never forget, and on that my first day I could never have envisaged, the joy, peace and sense of privilege I was to experience in that room with that view. In the years I was there I sat and watched the sea in its many different moods – stormy and calm. I remember distinctly the days when the sunlight caught the spray from the waves, making hundreds of miniature rainbows.

After that first day life was a bit of a haze as I tried to learn this new job and prepare for Christmas. Perhaps if I had known just what was required of me it would have put me off! I learnt that in the summer season I would be required to prepare and lead walks; prepare coach trips; and prepare and lead evenings' entertainment. Alongside that I would also need to step in at times when we had no Host

and Hostess, usually out of season, and lead the morning
and evening devotions. As the pre-Christmas preparations
were slowly revealed it seemed more and more daunting. I
had to prepare a Service for Christmas Eve. This would be
led by the Staff members with the guests as congregation.
As a Methodist Local Preacher on Trial that was not too
daunting, apart from the limited time to prepare it along
with everything else. Then I had to prepare two full days of
social activities for Christmas Day and Boxing Day and also
for New Year's Eve and New Year's Day, as well as some lesser
activities for the days in-between.

But as usual the Lord had prepared the way. Before I
had time to panic Marjorie Brown, the Manageress, suddenly announced shortly after I arrived that I had some
holiday owing! I was dumb-struck; I had hardly been there
two minutes! So off I went home to Irene's for a few days
and as soon as she knew what I had to do, especially in
terms of evening's entertainment, she produced numerous books of party games. Was there any end to the gifts
and abilities of this kind lady who had taken me under
her wing and now called me 'my little daughter'? Most of
that holiday at home was spent pouring over books and
discussing what I could do! By the time I was due back at
'Moorlands' I was armed with loads of ideas and felt more
fully prepared for what was in front of me. And of course
Irene had soaked the whole situation in prayer, so what
had I to fear?

Just before Christmas along came this little ditty just to
give me reassurance:

> May Christmas be a wondrous time,
> A time of peace and love,

Of making friends, of laughter,
Of shining star above,
Of going down to Bethlehem
And quietly kneeling there
And sharing in the worship
Of our Lord, beyond compare.

(Mum – Irene)

That first Christmas at 'Moorlands' was all of those things, and more. It was a baptism of fire! However I was extremely fortunate that the couple hosting were Roy and Joan, friends of Marjorie's who came each Christmas to act as Host and Hostess, and they were old hands at this. Without their generous-hearted help and advice I don't think I could possibly have coped, but the Lord knew what He was doing and placed the right people at my elbow at every turn.

For one who was an only child and who had always known fairly quiet Christmases, this one was tremendous. I was surrounded by lots of very loving Christians, who gathered together at this special time of year to fellowship together with God's people and to enjoy the celebration of what was indeed Christ's birthday. And what a party it was! There was an endless round of activities from Christmas Eve until into the beginning of the New Year, along with very late nights!

It was with mixed feelings that I waved goodbye to all the guests early in the New Year. I had made many new friends and there was the promise that I would see many of them again. However alongside that there was also a certain amount of relief that the pressure would ease off and I could begin to enjoy a steadier routine.

Now began a time of welcoming Conference and Church Party groups in for weekends, and also preparing for the summer season ahead. Again there was the joy of getting to know the groups and, as new friendships were formed, learning that the same ones would often come back year after year. It was also good to spend time in the office with Marjorie who patiently explained to me the kinds of things I needed to prepare for the summer ahead and gave me ideas to help me along. I also helped her with some of the general office work and when she knew my love of letter writing she gave me the task of writing her business letters, 'because you are good at it dear" she said. With regard to my job as Social Secretary, one of the main things important to understand was about the roads in the area which had very steep hills – some with gradients anywhere between 1 in 3 to 1 in 5. It was only after I had prepared what I thought was a good coach trip, calling at places of interest with the 'expected' stops for coffee and afternoon tea breaks, that Marjorie told me I had included a narrow road with a steep hill which was not safe for the coach to negotiate! Not long afterwards she very kindly spent several days taking me around the area in her car, showing me the steep hills; advising me on good places to stop for visits and refreshments; and generally helping me to see places and know where they were on the map. She was an absolute gem!

Many days were also taken up with going out into the countryside and finding new walks. There were sometimes full day walks on which I would be expected to lead a group whilst the Host and Hostess went off in a coach with the rest of the guests. Other walks would be prepared to fit in with the coach trips so that we would get off at a strategic point, walk for an hour or more, and then join up again with those on the coach for lunch and tea breaks together. I was again helped in my quest to find suitable walks in a countryside that was new to me. My first helper was Peter who had left school and was taking a gap year working at Moorlands before going to University. He loved walking, having come to 'Moorlands' with his parents for holidays over many years, so he knew the area well. Then there was Margaret the assistant cook, another young person very eager to help by going out walking with me on her days off during the week. With their help, and that of Marjorie, the programme for the summer season was finally prepared and drawn up. Coaches were booked, and chapels and other places were contacted to arrange stops for morning coffees, lunches and afternoon teas.

That first year was indescribably wonderful. Very full days were spent in the presence of many wonderful Christian people. As we travelled together either on foot or on the coach trips, and as we travelled together in fellowship, many deep and meaningful conversations of faith took place.

Sing a little song
As you walk along;
Say a little prayer
Breathe it on the air;
Smile a sunny smile
Another's woe beguile;
Lend a helping hand
Because you understand.
To everyone you see
God's messenger you'll be.

(Mum – Irene)

I found that the North York moors and Whitby and its surrounds boasted the most beautiful places, and I was privileged to visit so many, all as part of my job! During my time at 'Moorlands' I got to know every nook and cranny of so many quaint villages, and all the little gift shops selling a variety of interesting items. There was Lealholm nestling in a fold in the North York Moors, with its pretty garden centre, a fascinating working pottery, and a river with stepping stones where children paddled and families picnicked, At Glaisdale a wonderful old packhorse bridge held a fascinating love story which the guests loved to hear. Grosmont was a hub of activity as it was there that the North Yorks Moors Railway with its tourist steam trains joined tracks with the British Rail line from Middlesbrough to Whitby.

Goathland, where ITV's 'Heartbeat' is filmed, was visited often and there in the Parish Church were many carvings of the famous Robert Thompson, with their significant 'signature' of a carved mouse. Ruswarp, nestling by the river not far from Whitby, was a favourite place for afternoon teas at the tearooms beside the river. Many people were drawn to Robin Hood's Bay, whether on our coach trips or independently. It perched on the hillside on the coast just south of Whitby. It was distinctive for its cobbled road which led down to the sea, and the myriad little pathways off that road wending their way round pretty cottages bedecked in summer with hanging baskets and planters tumbling over with flowering sweet-smelling plants. Hutton-le-Hole boasted a superb folk museum, being old cottages set around a village green.

It was possible to walk to Sandsend on the coast just north of Whitby and this was reached along the mile or two of beautiful golden sands almost from the door of Moorlands (after descending the cliff path first, of course!). Runswick

Bay, north of Whitby was a small hamlet situated at the bottom of a 1 in 3 hill and its cottages hugged the coastline. This was a place which attracted artists and one could find many paintings and line-drawings of Runswick in the shops around the area. Staithes, just north of Whitby, was once a thriving fishing village and it was here that Captain James Cook was once apprenticed. A house still has a plaque to that effect.

In Danby village sheep roamed along all the roads, so each dwelling in the village had a cattle grid at the entrance to its drive to stop the sheep wandering in and eating all their garden shrubs! To be found outside the village was Danby Lodge – the North York Moors Visitor Centre – a fascinating place with plenty grounds outside for picnicking and for the children to play. Lastingham once earned itself the title of 'the prettiest village in England' and it boasted a lovely country church with a fascinating crypt. Here, on a very hot day, we would descend into the crypt via the steps and find a cool and spiritually refreshing place to sit and quietly reflect. Thornton-le-Dale had its famous thatched cottage often seen on calendars and chocolate boxes. A stream ran alongside the village streets with footbridges across to the cottages. This was a really popular place with tourists, its car and coach parking almost always full and the village buzzing with people. All these places and many more were entrancing, and however many times I visited I never got tired of them.

Apart from the obvious plug for Whitby and the North York moors, I hope the reader will understand my desire to convey how gracious the Lord had been in bringing me to this area. The visits to the above places, along with the wonderful Christian fellowship, were all part of His very gracious Plan for me, His child.

The visits to little country chapels for morning coffee, with our packed lunch, or for afternoon tea, were great, and again new friendships were formed amongst their members. We were allowed to play the organ in some Chapels we visited. If we had an organist among us we would have singsongs round the organ over our refreshments. The fellowship was superb and on the rainy or dull days we were often lifted beyond the realms of the 'here and now' as for a short while we praised God together round the organ. All of these were very bonding experiences between myself, the guests, and the local Christians.

Initially the hardest part for me was the evening entertainment. Members of staff were extremely kind in telling me what kind of things had been done by previous Social Secretaries and I took some of those ideas on board and used them. I also replicated some of the fun quizzes I had seen on television and these, to my great surprise, turned out to be most successful and extremely funny. The guests, being generous-hearted Christians, made the very best of all my efforts to entertain them, joining in with great enthusiasm. They dressed up as children and mimicked them, they were extremely intelligent in replicating TV quiz shows, and managed to make everything most laughable and real good fun. However when it came to leading country dancing, I kept making mistakes and got everybody in a tangle, especially in dances like 'Red River Valley' where one had to weave in and out and keep changing partners. I became very frustrated and felt inadequate and often near to tears. However I found that the guests laughed a lot at the dances that went wrong and if I laughed with them and turned my mistakes into a joke it went down tremendously. Suddenly I found that I had been gifted a comedienne and I used it for all I was worth! The ice was broken and I stopped feeling such a fool. After a while people seemed not to realise that the mistakes were actually real but began to think that it was part of the entertainment plan! I even pretended things went wrong when they didn't and it worked like a dream!

Give me a sense of humour Lord,
In all things, great or small,
Help me to laugh instead of cry
That my spirits do not fall.
Teach me to note the pleasant things
As I pass along life's way,
Above all, Lord, just guide my tongue
And watch the words I say.
Fill me with love and joyfulness,
A giggle now and then,
So others see You as I pass
And turn to You again.
Make me Your messenger, dear Lord
And when I slip, I pray
You'll lift me up to start again
To walk Your precious Way.

(Mum – Irene)

So finally summer drew to a close, guests drifted away, and Whitby became a different place altogether. I had time to enjoy the town and to explore it more, and by this time I had fallen in love with it. Whitby sits on a hillside with the lower town and the upper town. Quaint buildings cluster on the hillside, and down in the bottom of the town are the shops, the marina, and the fishing harbour crossed by a road bridge which lifts occasionally to allow the boats to pass under. Crossing the bridge over the River Esk from the harbour and wandering along the streets, one arrives at the bottom of the 199 steps leading up to the top of the cliffs where St Mary's Church and Whitby Abbey stand resplendent. The Church is fascinating with its box pews, and the holders for the candles which to this very day are the only light source in the Church. I well remember a wonderful schools' Christmas Service when the candlelight and the sound of children's voices gave it a certain kind of magic. The air in Whitby is fresh and clear and very bracing, and the cry of the seagulls is constant. Not everyone enjoys the air as it is very soporific and makes everyone sleep at first. However this is ideal for those who come to Whitby exhausted, needing to rest and to sleep well. As for the seagulls – well some of us love the sound, one just has to be sure to dodge them so as not to get 'dropped on'! In later years I was surprised one day to find myself penning the following about my love of Whitby. Surprised because although I loved writing I had never thought of writing poetry. To this day this is the only poem I have ever written, although it can never be as good as dear Irene's...

VIRGINIA HAYWOOD

'I fell in love with Whitby
One summer, years ago,
That fair and balmy place
Where the tides do ebb and flow.

It happened quite unusually
As I prayed for a new job,
And Jesus heard my prayer
And my heart-rending sob.

He called on me to 'follow',
And he promised nought but good;
For all who heed the bidding
He brings the flower to bud.

The train it trundled gently
Along the valley track,
And I quietly reflected
That there was no turning back.

But as the train neared Whitby
And the sea came into view,
A sense of peace descended,
And in my heart it grew

This was a new beginning,
The past was left behind,
And Jesus whispered gently
"New treasures you will find".

It was a place of beauty,
Of warmth and kindness, too,

A place where hearts were loving,
  And folks were kind and true.

A place much steeped in history,
  Where many saints have trod
    The pathways of obedience
  On their daily walk with God.

    It boasts of dear St Hilda,
      Patron of poor and ill,
    Who, as she tended lovingly,
      Carried out God's will.

    Many were the people
  Who helped to shape this place,
  And as they worked so tirelessly
    God gave of His free grace.

    But what of today's Whitby,
  And the folk who work and play
    And serve the many tourists
      Who go there day by day?

There's fishermen, and landlords,
    Hoteliers by the score,
  Shopkeepers, and entertainers,
    Who make you ask for more.

  They make the summer lively,
      At Whitby by the sea,
  Drawing many people to them:
      And that included me!

                    (Virginia Haywood)

I was thrilled and privileged that the Lord had brought me to this place, that in some small way I was following in ancient footsteps of service, and receiving life in all its fullness.

CHAPTER NINE

RELATIONSHIPS

'no-one who has left home or brothers or sisters or mother or father...for me and for the gospel, will fail to receive a hundred times as much in this present age . . brothers, sisters, mothers' (Mark 10 : 29-30)

IN THIS WONDERFUL new job it was great to meet so many new people, to make new friends, and year in and year out to renew those friendships. My spiritual life was so richly enhanced by the friendships I made and through the conversations I held with the guests. If I am being honest it was the most spiritually enriching part of my life to date. Also the 'quiet Virginia' who had been shy and retiring all her life was enabled to come out of her shell and to interact with these people. I glowed with a new vitality. This was something I would never have dreamed possible a few years ago. There was a definite sense of God equipping me for the task, but the instruments He used for this work were the people I met and the people I worked with.

I had a very solitary childhood. I was the only child of a couple who were married in mid-life and so it was highly unlikely that my mother would bear another child. I remember when very young asking her if I could have a brother or sister and being very disappointed when it never happened. I was quite ill as a young child, missing a great deal of schooling and, when not in hospital, spending a lot of time at home with my mother. Therefore there was little or no interaction with other children of my own age and I suppose I got used to a solitary lifestyle and my own company.

As a result of this the Staff at 'Moorlands' became very special to me. There was a very close bond between us all, and we were like one large family. Marjorie, the Manageress, was like the mother figure. She was a good lady to have around, and always had words of wisdom in times of difficulty. She could be strict when it was necessary but underneath was a heart of gold – a heart which was soft and loving. The rest of the staff became like brothers and sisters to me, and there were many of them. Kathleen, the cook, lived in and I will mention her in more depth in a short while. Margaret, her assistant, lived locally and came in daily. She was in her late teens and when I arrived she was doing day release at College in Scarborough in connection with her work, so I only saw her in short snatches. We did, however, strike up a great friendship and she was most helpful to me in seeking out walks, and in other ways you will read of later. Margaret was flamboyant and was associated with the local amateur dramatic society, which perhaps explained her really interesting personality.

Janet (known as Little Janet for some reason – perhaps her small stature) worked in the kitchen as a general helper. She was quieter than the other staff but had hidden depths that others didn't always see or appear to know of. Besides working full-time in the kitchen – a difficult job – like me she was also a 'preacher on trial' in the Methodist Church. She spent most of her evenings locked away in her room (she also 'lived in') studying and preparing for services. Some of the staff looked upon her as unsociable but one had to admire her commitment to her 'call to preach' and the fact that she was willing to give up much of her social life to follow this 'call'. I think she struggled with her preaching studies, and possibly had problems we were unaware of, but the first time I heard her preach I was amazed at her capabilities. It was obvious she had read and researched a lot in order to present as she did. I felt very proud to know her.

Chris (Christopher) was the only full-time permanent male live-in member of staff but was a good chap to have around, working on the general domestic staff but being very good at all kinds of jobs. He had a great guffaw of a laugh and kept us all amused, although there was a much softer side to him too. Surprisingly he was a wonderful knitter and made some fantastic knitted garments. He was really good with old people, which was great in the spring and autumn when we tended to get coach loads of old people holidaying from Monday to Friday. They loved him.

Heather, in her late teens, was a vibrant person, always full of energy. She also worked on the general domestic staff and lived in. She was wonderfully gifted in craftworks, making all manner of beautiful items for friends and family. I once thought that had she had the resources and the will she could have opened up her own craft shop and filled it with her beautiful hand-made goods. She didn't – going on later in life to work with children and old people. We didn't hit it off too well when we worked together and it was a long time before I began to understand the possible reason why this might be. Heather apparently had applied unsuccessfully for the job of Social Secretary, which had eventually been given to me. I guess that as a much younger person (I was then 40) she perhaps thought she could have done the job much better than I. She probably could! I struggled immensely with my working relationship with Heather, but surprisingly when I eventually left Moorlands she was one of the few people to regularly and faithfully keep in contact with me and I have been touched by that. I remember once standing by Heather as we were practising for a Service we were to hold in Moorlands. We were singing 'Let there be peace on earth' and as I glanced at Heather the words we were singing really hit home. They were:

Let there be peace on earth
And let it begin with me...

It struck me very forcibly that even in relationships such as ours, working in close proximity, peace in that situation had to begin with me doing my best to make peace with Heather. What hope was there for the world if we couldn't even get on together as Christian brothers and sister in this close-knit community.

The Assistant Manageress, Freda, was also a motherly type. She had red hair (and sometimes the temperament which went with it!) but was a very able person and a wonderful help to Marjorie. I didn't get so close to Freda due to being out with the guests all day most days. Freda was a busy person with lots of other interests so our paths didn't cross as often as with other members of staff. However Freda had a good head on her shoulders, always knew how to help and advise staff on a myriad of matters, and was always interesting to listen to with her wealth of knowledge and stories of the things she had done in life.

Brenda was nearer my age, lived in, and was an absolute poppet. She had a singing voice like a nightingale and you would often hear her from afar, singing many popular songs or songs from the shows. She was always giggling and had such a happy personality and I loved her to bits. Then there was Margaret who came in on a daily basis. She was a very devout Roman Catholic. She was a quiet, gentle, and reflective person, and a good person to be around. I would often see her on her knees scrubbing floors or brushing corners of the carpets and in my mind's eye I could picture her as a nun, quietly and obediently doing that which was necessary with a good grace. Margaret was always there to talk to and would give quiet and considered replies if one asked her advice.

Edith was a staff member who came in several days a week and was another motherly type. She was always so cheerful and always there to talk to if one had a problem. Her husband Tom, although quite disabled, used to come regularly to tidy up the garden around 'Moorlands'. Together they made a great team and were a real asset.

Virginia, Brenda, Freda and Kathleen

VIRGINIA HAYWOOD

There were several other staff who came in during
the summer season, usually students who came during
their summer break in order to earn some money. Most of
them had connections with Moorlands in the sense that
they and their families had holidayed there in the past
and had a great attachment and loyalty to the place. As I
get older several names evade me, although I do remember Janet and her sister Joy; Katie; Peter and his sister
Frances; Miles, Julie, Robin. They were a super crowd of
young folk and the rest of the year was never quite the
same when they went back to College/University. Students will be students and they made life interesting and
full of laughs but couldn't do enough to help guests and
full-time staff. They were really good to have around.

In my early days at 'Moorlands' I struggled, as did
young Janet, with doing my job alongside the studying
for being a Local Preacher. My 'on trial' period lasted
rather a long time due to my long and unsocial hours of
work (sometimes 14 hour days) and the lack of available
time for studying. This had also been the case in my last
job. However the staff were fantastic in that they were a
mine of information when I was searching for subjects on
which to write sermons, or for illustrations. They were
always there and willing to be 'tapped' for information
on all kinds of things on which I had ideas. We would sit
around in the Staff Room 'chewing the cud' on all kinds
of subjects, and their discussions helped me greatly. For
quite a long time they were also very supportive in following me around wherever I preached, provided that
they could have the time off work on a Sunday morning.
Marjorie was very good in that sense and tried her best to
see that staff who wished to attend worship had the op-

portunity to do so. I didn't wish to see myself as a 'popular preacher' but I was most pleased and grateful at their commitment to supporting me, and it surely helped to swell the small congregations in the rural villages when we turned up en bloc! It was like 'rent a congregation'! This sense of 'family' had a great effect on my life.

Other relationships were with those who came to 'Host' the holiday weeks. They were absolute gems as far as I was concerned and, particularly in the early days, I don't know what I would have done without them. In my role of preparing and leading walks, coach trips, and evening entertainment, the Host and Hostess played a supportive role and helped to share the burden. Although I cannot now remember names I can picture in my mind's eye most of the couples who came for two-week slots and who, despite the short space of time, became very precious to me in my work. They were quite different to each other and the hardest thing was to adjust to another couple every 2 weeks during the summer season. On very rare occasions it didn't work out too well to start with, but by this time I had learnt to commit everything to God in prayer and, being a faithful God, in no time at all we found ourselves adjusting to each other and working well.

One very memorable moment in terms of relationships with the Hosts and Hostesses remains forever in my mind. On what must have been a quiet day during mid-summer the two persons hosting that 2-week session told me they would like to take me out for the afternoon. What a treat! I went to so many lovely places in this privileged job but it was usually me taking other people and it was often very exhausting rounding people up for walks, coaches, and doing the courier bit on the coach with stories about the countryside we were passing through, etc. To be taken out by someone else and allowed to sit back and just enjoy the scenery was absolute bliss.

So off we set. It was a beautiful, hot sunny day and I sat in the back of the car with the window down, hair blowing in the breeze. My cardigan was open and although warm the breeze got a little too much for me. As I put my hand out to draw my cardigan closed, I felt a terrible stinging sensation. Unknown to me a bee had flown in through the window and inside my blouse. As I had put my hand up to pull my cardigan closed over my blouse it must have thought I was going to attack it. I cried out; the car skid to a halt – wonderful emergency stop – and Olivia jumped out, flung my door open, grabbed my hand and hurriedly sucked the bee sting from my thumb! Having since learnt the danger of bee stings causing anaphylactic shock to some people one could almost ask the question 'did she save my life?' That was the only day I was ever taken out, and it ended with a bee sting and a large white bandage wrapped round my throbbing thumb!

One of the best, if not **the** best, relationships formed during my time at 'Moorlands' was with Kathleen, the Cook. Kathleen visited me briefly in my room on the day I first arrived, to say 'welcome'. Our conversation was a little stilted. I was new and a little shy and Kathleen (as I later found out) was also shy with people she didn't know. As the months went by we started to become closer, especially due to our interest in music. Kathleen could play guitar well and although I had taken my guitar with me I wasn't too brilliant, certainly not as good as she. Very slowly a special relationship developed between us, and it was like having the sister I had always longed for. We be-

gan to share our love of music by singing and playing together, and as time progressed we entertained the guests
in this way. Kathleen and I also shared fellowship together, having serious talks about the Bible and our faith, and
at one point in time we even started a small Bible Study
in the house. Sometimes we would go walking together
and, like others before her, she also came with me on occasions to help me find new walks for the guests. It was
good to have all these very special relationships with so
many different people, and they were so very life-enrich-
ing, but the friendship with Kathleen was extra special.

Kathleen

Some of the relationships I had with guests were funny. It
was a well-known hazard of a female unattached Social Secretary that unattached males made a bee-line for you! They
seemed to attach great importance to making friends with
the Social Secretary. Oftentimes they assumed they were the
'bees-knees' (no offence to bees intended) and that they were

the most important thing in a Social Secretary's life! This could get quite difficult at times as I often had 30+ people to look after; to be nice and attentive to; to ensure were on the coach and not left behind; and had not been missed out when the morning coffee or the tea and scones were served, etc! Under these circumstances personal attention to one or more unattached males was difficult and inappropriate, to say the least!

These brief interludes, although sometimes irritating, were great fun, but I always had to try and include these males in the social activity going on in order that they didn't take over completely and monopolise me to the exclusion of my attention to other guests. One particular way of doing this was during the evening when we read our Noddy Bedtime Stories! It was a longstanding tradition at 'Moorlands' to read Noddy stories at bedtime – no, not to the children, but to the adults! People sat on the stairs and clustered in groups around the bottom of the stairs in the Entrance Hall, and the Social Secretary read one of the stories. At some point in the past someone had provided hats appropriate to the characters in the stories, and so we had to find a Noddy, a Mr Plod the policeman, and Big Ears etc, and persuade them to wear the hats! I decided to go one better and slowly introduced the acting out of the stories by the guests, as I read the stories. I would not have been seen dead doing what I asked the guests to do but, with book in my hands, I managed to persuade the male of the species to act out the story as I sat reading it! This was usually an opportunity to include those men of a certain age to shine, and they managed to feel special because they had been picked out for these roles by the Social Secretary! This usually placated them and they then left me alone during the day, looking forward to their special role during the evening! It was fun and it was harmless, and it solved a problem into the bargain.

One evening as we had just started to read and act out a particular Noddy story there was a ring at the front doorbell. One of our party opened the door to find a young American lady there. She was staying in a Guest House a few doors down and had heard the laughter. She posed the question 'was it a private 'do' or could she join us?' Being kind Christians we invited her in and tried to explain what we were doing. She was bemused at these antics of the English, to say the least! Trying to make the best of the situation I asked loudly and jokingly "perhaps you have heard about our Amateur Dramatics Group and decided to come and see how good we are? You wouldn't happen to be from Hollywood, would you?" Quite seriously she replied "yes I am"! You can imagine the laughter which ensued this mat-ter-of-fact reply. We thought at first she was joking but found out that she did indeed live in Hollywood. In future weeks and months we made great play on the fact that we had been visited by someone from Hollywood who had been to give our Noddy dramatics the once-over with a view to making a film!

Left to right – Big Ears, Noddy, Virginia, and Mr Plod

So time flew by and many friendships were cemented amongst both the staff and the guests, and life was wonderful. My request as a child for a brother or sister had now been answered a hundredfold by these people who had now become my family in Christ. And in the centre of it all was Jesus Christ, guiding and equipping me for my work, but also bringing great joy and enrichment through my relationships with each one.

CHAPTER TEN

A CHANGING FUTURE

**'One more step along the world I go
One more step along the world I go
From the old things to the new
Keep me travelling along with You'**

(Hymns & Psalms No 746)

WHEN I GOT the job at 'Moorlands' I felt such great peace about going there and was so very happy in the job. I was sure that this was to be my 'calling' for the rest of my working life. I never envisaged that there would be any other job in my life nor that I would move on again until retirement. But all that was to change.

Following the comments in the last chapter about the succession of men of a certain age who made a beeline for me, I never seriously anticipated that I would have a serious relationship with a man again, and certainly not re-marry. Despite my innocence in my former marriage break-up I did still carry a certain amount of guilt around with me – justified or not – and did not believe that as a Christian I would be worthy of marrying again; didn't even know how the Lord would view that. It took a great deal of counselling from a few very kind guests, amongst them Local Preachers and Methodist Ministers, to get me to the point where I felt that Christ would not condemn me but would allow this to happen at some point in the future if it was indeed right and within His will. They helped me to understand that God wills the very best for His people but that He doesn't (metaphorically speaking) stand with a big stick in His hand towering over us and warning us never to seek for happiness again. He wills for us to be freed from those things which mar His purpose for us. To those who helped me through their exposition of the Scriptures on this matter I am eternally grateful.

One week in the summer of 1985 the requirements on me as Social Secretary did not follow the usual trend. It was August and despite a house full of people there were only four (all males) who wanted to go on the prepared walks. This was most unusual and Marjorie did say I could take the day off. It would have been easy to opt out of the responsibility for the walks and do my own thing and take a rest but this was my job and it hardly seemed appropriate to take time off for myself if four of them wished to walk. So off we set. Although only four guests it took me a little time to get to know them and to feel comfortable in conversation, especially as they were of the opposite sex.

After a while, and although we often walked as a group and conversed together, I drifted into conversation more frequently with one of the group on a one to one basis, possibly because his conversation was more theological and I found that both interesting and helpful. I do not now remember whether I told him of my divorce and my concerns about remarriage, or whether this general subject just came up in conversation, but he told me at great length about the pastorally caring and sensitive view of this particular issue which had been taken by the former well-known cricketer David Sheppard, then ordained and serving in Liverpool Cathedral. I found this more helpful than anything I had heard to date and it gave me a new perspective and a new hope.

This young man, Denis, was a most interesting person to talk with. He was currently employed and lived on the premises of Cliff College in Derbyshire. This was a Methodist Lay Training College. I had heard much about this place but had never visited. When I was in my teens, my friends from the Methodist Church I attended often went there as a group at Whitsuntide, but I could not attend with them – my parents being very poor. When I was living for a time with Irene and Joe they talked often of Cliff College. They had long connections with the place as Irene's sister had married Joe Blinco, one of Cliff College's Evangelists who later became part of the Billy Graham Team, and Irene and Joe had been to Cliff College regularly over many years and right up to the present time.

As we walked Denis talked much of Cliff, which was most interesting. He also spoke of his hopes and dreams for his own future. He felt a call to the Methodist Ministry but sadly found it difficult to pass his O level in English – this being a requirement of entrance for the candidating procedure. Many years later it became evident that his problem stemmed from dyslexia which, at that time, he was unaware of. Despite the difficulties he was anxious to keep on trying, and as we talked

I began to admire him greatly for his faith, and for his persistence to follow God's will for his life. There was a kind of attractiveness towards him because of Christ in his life – a kind of attractiveness I had never experienced before.

At the end of his week holiday we parted by exchanging addresses and promised to keep in touch, and I felt I had made a really good friend. We wrote several times afterwards and it became a really precious friendship as we shared much through letter-writing. Several months later I heard that Revd Howard Mellor, Director of Evangelism at Cliff College, was to visit and speak at our Methodist Church in Whitby, so I wrote to Denis and asked whether he might be able to take the opportunity to come along with Revd Mellor. The response was 'yes' and I looked forward to meeting up again with this new friend and to continuing our conversations.

The day arrived and Howard Mellor dropped Denis off at 'Moorlands' where we had tea together in my room and talked about his family and all manner of other things. So engrossed were we in conversation of things we shared in common that we suddenly realised that it was time to make our way to the church for Revd Mellor's talk. We arrived a little late – the meeting having begun – and there were certain amused smiles on some faces which I found hard to understand. How naïve I was! When the meeting was over and we went outside to say our goodbyes it had started to snow. Suddenly I found that this new male friend was kissing me goodbye, and a warm glow filled my whole being. I walked back to 'Moorlands' as if walking on air, and suddenly realised that this friendship was turning into something else. This was most unexpected and yet as I reflected on past months I ought to have seen it coming. During my quiet times of reading the Bible, and since the helpful talks by kind friends about marriage, much of my Scripture readings had made mention of marrying; of man and woman; of two being better than one, if one fell the other could help the other up, and so on. I suddenly felt that God had been preparing me for this moment.

As I walked into 'Moorlands' that evening my mind went back to the week Denis came on holiday, and to a momentary forgotten incident which I must have pushed to the back of my mind. On the first Sunday of his week with us, as usual I led a group of those who wanted to attend the Methodist Church service through the streets of Whitby to the Church. By pure chance I sat alongside Denis. As we stood singing a hymn during the Service, I glanced at Denis whose face was rapturous as he worshipped God, lifting his hands in praise, and a still small voice whispered in my mind 'you're going to marry this man'. Shock horror! What **was** I thinking? I'd only met him the day before when he arrived with all the other guests. 'Don't be silly, Virginia' I told myself and shook myself inwardly, scandalised at my thought. Then just as suddenly I realised that my mind of its own will had not said '**I'm** going to marry this man'. The words were from a second party – '**you're** going to marry this man'. I finally realised that this must be God speaking to me. It was hard to take in.

Thinking back to the time we had spent together during Denis's holiday and mostly the walking times, I realised that in those conversations God had been drawing us together in Him, showing us what we had in common and how we complemented each other. But the kiss that night in winter, outside the Methodist Church in Whitby, that was the seal – the beginning – of something preordained by God. I am reminded of the kiss mentioned in that wonderful Welsh Revival hymn where it states 'Grace and love like mighty rivers poured incessant from above, and heaven's peace and perfect justice kissed a guilty world in love'. Whatever I had done in the past, whoever I had been, God's grace and love was being poured out in great measure, and the kiss of Denis was as if a kiss from God, kissing away my sins and offering me a new start. From that moment on I started to pray in earnest about Denis. In prayer many times I had already asked the Lord that if it was His perfect will or His permissive will that I marry again, to please not allow me to meet anyone who was not a Christian: if there was ever to be a next time I desperately wanted to share my life with someone who loved Him as I did – that we might share our faith together. In the state of grace in which I now stood this was of vital importance.

One day I knelt in my small bedroom overlooking the sea and prayed to God. I was so unsure of His will about Denis, and my feelings for him were growing very strong. I was agonising about these feelings. So I prayed 'Lord if it is not Your will for me to love Denis or to share my life with Him, then please take away these feelings I now have for him, and don't allow it to happen and don't let us see each other again' or words to that effect. I had hardly said the prayer and said 'amen' before there was tap on the door. It was Valerie, the new Assistant Manageress, with the cordless phone in her hand. "Virginia, it's Denis for you". My heart leaped with an indescribable joy. When I took the phone from Valerie, Denis's first words to me were "I'm ringing to ask what you feel about you and I". Many years afterwards I cannot remember the exact con-versation which then took place but as we talked it be-came clear to us that God had been working in both our hearts and minds and we both felt He wanted us to make our lives together.

After that initial decision the actual courtship process was difficult. Denis was doing a job that took up many hours and with little time off. This mirrored mine, which was virtually 6 days a week requirement, usually from the time I got up until the time I locked the Hotel door at 11-11.30 pm at night after the guests had retired to bed. My one day off during the week was spent mostly trying to do my Local Preacher 'on trial' studies which, due to living on two successive jobs with long and unsocial hours, were now way behind. However the Lord was present even in these seemingly impossible circumstances.

CHAPTER ELEVEN

NOTHING IS IMPOSSIBLE FOR GOD

'If you have faith as small as a mustard seed. . . nothing will be impossible for you'. (Matthew 17 : 20)

DESPITE THE DIFFICULTIES of time and distance, things worked amazingly for us to get together and get to know each other better. Denis had a Departmental Head – Edna the Matron – who was an absolute treasure and who insisted on many occasions that he should have time off in lieu of the many extra hours he had worked. This allowed Denis to visit me now and again in Whitby, a wonderful place for courtship!

The first time was when he had to take some students on mission to a place north of Whitby and he decided to stop off on the way back to see me. Due to Matron's allowing him to take that extra time he was able to stop off overnight at Moorlands. This enabled him to have a very necessary rest instead of driving all the way back to Derbyshire on the same day, and we had a little time to spend with each other.

On this occasion he was almost collapsing with extreme tiredness and the opportunity to stop off and see me and have a rest was really necessary to his health and well-being. Another time he had been invited to the wedding of a former student friend. This also was not many miles north of Whiby and when, at the last minute, the friend knew Denis was courting me I was invited to the wedding. This enabled Denis to spend the whole weekend at Whitby, and both of us to enjoy the wedding and our time together. At the wedding the Lord gave us very specific words about joining our lives. These were from the hymn 'All Praise to our Redeeming Lord' and the specific words which stood out to us were:

'All praise to our Redeeming Lord
who joins us by His grace,
And bids us, each to each restored,
Together seek His face.
He bids us build each other up;
And gathered into one,
To our high calling's glorious hope
We hand in hand go on.'

There were many opportunities for courtship presented to us, and Whitby became a very special 'courting place'. Not only did it allow us the very necessary time to spend together and get to know each other but it also gave Denis equally necessary times apart from his very demanding work.

It was during this time of our courtship that Marjorie was taken ill and had to go into hospital. At first it seemed touch and go whether she would recover and there were even fears that she might die. As the Assistant Manageress had recently retired and no replacement had yet been found I was given the task of taking over the office side of the Manageress's work – Acting Manageress – and holding all things together. I was ably assisted by my dear friend, Kathleen the cook, who before working in the kitchen had been on the housekeeping side. She was able to continue her everyday role whilst also ably taking the Housekeepers position. Although all of us worked much longer hours we all pulled together and the work was adequately completed.

Fortunately during the winter months I had worked alongside Marjorie and knew how to do most of the office work and, as I mentioned in an earlier chapter, she often asked me to do letters for her as she felt this was a particular gift of mine. I enjoyed doing the office work – had spent much of my life doing just that anyway – and a young man was found to take over my social secretary role.

Other dear friends of Moorlands took time out occasionally to come and help us voluntarily. Robin was the boyfriend of Julie, one of our regular summer student helpers who by now had taken time out from University to help on a more full-time basis. Robin came as often as he could to help Julie and the whole situation. Denis also visited and helped a little voluntarily as often as his time-off from work at the College permitted. This pulling together in times of need drew the staff much closer together but also helped to knit together our individual relationships. Denis and I enjoyed our times of helping together and it created a closeness which perhaps would not have been so strong without this particular crisis. It certainly paved the way for our future, when we would find ourselves in situations living and working 'on the job' together.

During this time I tentatively asked the staff if they would be willing to meet together with me for a very brief time to pray for Marjorie as her illness was taking its time and progress was very slow. We still feared for her future health. At first only a handful of staff came but as time went on just about everyone gave up 5 minutes or so of their morning coffee time to pray for Marjorie. This was most encouraging. Then this prayer for Marjorie extended and we started to pray about other situations and about each other and eventually the prayer time became a real powerhouse. Staff (some not even Christians) actually became willing to give up their morning coffee break altogether in order to spend time in prayer with each other, yet the work never suffered as a result. We began to see God honouring our prayer time. During this time there was a crisis in some of the Guild Hotels, and there were fears that some might have to close down if guest numbers/bookings didn't improve. Moorlands was one of the places experiencing low bookings and we were all extremely concerned. It wasn't just a case of being concerned for our jobs – we loved the place and all it stood for. We started to tell people about this and to ask for their prayers – people at our local Churches, guests who came, those who came to act as Hosts, and many others. We also made it an item for prayer at our now regular staff prayer meetings. As the weeks and months went by, and we and others prayed, guest bookings started to pick up, and as they did so all of us were made aware of how God intervenes for the good of all when we start to commune with Him and include Him in every aspect of our lives. Even personal prayers for the problems of staff members were answered in abundance. It was a wonderful learning curve about the Lord's ability to work in any situation, however desperate it might seem, and to see how situations were turned around so that they worked for the good of all.

CHAPTER TWELVE

TIME TO MOVE ON

'Jesus said, "Do not let your heart be troubled. Trust in God, trust also in me. . .I go to prepare a place for you' (John 14 : 1)

I MENTIONED EARLIER that I thought when I arrived at 'Moorlands that this was to be for the rest of my working life. However matters conspired against me and it soon became apparent this was not to be. Before I met Denis I had already started to suffer with what were termed 'tension headaches' (now I know their correct term is 'muscle contraction headaches') and as time went by they became unbearable. At their very worst my head felt as if it was being held in a vice which was slowly but surely being tightened, and at times I could barely hold a conversation. Being with the guests all day long every day was becoming more than I could bear. The constant conversations, entertaining, and particularly making polite and interesting conversations over meals was excruciating. I didn't know what to do for the best. When Marjorie went into hospital and my job changed, some of the pressure was taken off when the lack of continual 'giving out' in conversation to guests was not now as intense, and for a while I was much better.

Eventually I went to the doctor and was told that this problem was stress-related and that I must either reduce my working hours or leave my job. I could not reduce my hours – that was the work – and to leave my job, oh dear. I was devastated at the thought. It was at this time that Mum Irene penned yet another of her lovely poems:

We cannot know the way ahead
We cannot see the path to tread
But we can feel that we are lead
By Jesus Christ, our Lord.

We know not what the day will bring
But as we walk His song we'll sing
And as we trust in everything
We'll praise our loving Lord.

We know our times are in His Hand,
Upon the Rock of Faith we'll stand
And trust, when we can't understand,
In Jesus, Loving Lord.

How wonderful it is to know
That where through life our path may go,
So also He, who loves us so,
Walks with us, – Jesus – Lord!

The thought of leaving my job became more of a reality when Denis and I became closer and felt that the Lord was telling us to share our lives. Both of us were in single person's jobs that provided single person's accommodation, so when we finally decided to marry it seemed that the only way was for us both to leave our respective jobs and start again somewhere else. For a while there had been the hope that I might be invited to take over as Manageress at Moorlands, and that idea was put to me on several occasions by a former Social Secretary who was now in a more senior position within the Company. But whilst I would have liked that, and Denis and I could perhaps have had married accommodation at Moorlands, it wasn't long before a new Assistant Manageress was appointed and, in Marjorie's absence, took over for a while as Manager. Any ideas that I might have had for this position were now quashed. I was quite disappointed but it now became plain that my time at Moorlands was coming to a close, but what might have otherwise been a bitter and very sad pill to swallow was sweetened considerably by the thought of starting a new life with Denis. The words of a hymn had been running through my mind repeatedly for some time and they now seemed to apply to this situation. They are the words from some of the verses of the hymn 'God moves in a mysterious way' – to be found as number 65 in Methodism's Hymns and Psalms:-

> Deep in unfathomable mines
> Of never failing skill
> He treasures up His bright designs
> And works His sovereign will.

Ye fearful saints fresh courage take,
The clouds ye so much dread
Are big with blessing, and shall break
In blessings on your head.

Judge not the Lord by feeble sense,
But trust Him for His grace;
Behind a frowning providence
He hides a smiling face.

His purposes will ripen fast,
Unfolding every hour;
The bud may have a bitter taste,
But sweet will be the flower.

Blind unbelief is sure to err,
And scan His work in vain;
God is His own interpreter,
And He will make it plain.

(Hymns & Psalms 65)

Despite all the difficulties things were indeed working out for the good of ourselves and others.

CHAPTER THIRTEEN

GOD'S INFINITE RESOURCES OF GRACE

'Therefore I tell you do not worry about your life, what you will eat...what you will wear. . .Your Father knows you need these thing. . .' (Luke 12 : 22-31)

ALTHOUGH THERE WAS a definite proposal from Denis and which took place in the lovely park not far from the Church where we eventually married, (and which became the place for our wedding photos) nevertheless it was more of a joint decision that we knew our lives were meant to be spent together, and an agreement that this was to join our lives in marriage. It was wonderful to be marrying a man who had such a wonderful Christian faith that together we could share. Denis was also a Methodist Local Preacher, so we had that in common too, and he helped me enormously with my preaching studies as a local preacher in training, and with thoughts and ideas on sermons.

My time at Moorlands was drawing to a close, hastened on by the stress-related 'headache' problem, but the Lord had so graciously taken care of that by giving me such a lovely way of drawing out of that situation. Who would have ever dreamed that He would have resolved it by marriage!

We set the date for 23rd August 1986 – only 1 year after we had originally met and started a relationship by becoming firm friends. As the time drew nearer we started to worry about what we were both to do. Looking back I realise how very brave and how very trusting we were in setting a date for marrying without having a home and jobs, and I don't know if I would be brave and trusting enough do the same now as I did those 20 years ago. But circumstances dictate how one acts and at that time there was no other way. Denis and I found ourselves trusting the Lord completely in this and He was to show us how utterly trustworthy He was.

As it got nearer to the wedding there was so much to do. Not only were there wedding preparations to make but also the additional matter of a home and jobs for one or both of us. Little seemed to be available in terms of a job with a home to go with it and neither of us had much money due to working in Christian service jobs with low pay, so buying or even renting a home was entirely out of the question. By pure chance (or was it?) these circumstances coincided with the fact that I had recently sent out my usual Easter Newsletters to many friends all over the country. However some of these had not been received by friends in the Leeds area owing to a Postal Strike where post boxes had been sealed up. One of the people I still kept in contact with was the Social Worker from the Jewish Housing Association in Leeds. One day I received an unexpected telephone call from her work. The post boxes in Leeds had just been unsealed and she had received my Newsletter. This told about Denis coming into my life and about our efforts to find a home and a job. She told me that the person who had been the Assistant Warden for the Sheltered Housing Scheme where I had been Warden had just left due to illness and asked whether I might be interested in going back there, to Green Park, as the Assistant Warden. The pay was very low, but there was the flat offered rent free, along with free electricity, free use of telephone, etc, as before. I could hardly believe it!

Denis and I went along for an interview and they seemed delighted to offer me the job again although were at great pains to explain that there was only the one job and it was for me. We understood that and were delighted to accept. This meant that we would have a home, no overheads to pay, and a small income which, along with Denis's money from signing on for work, would help us to cope until he could find work. Also the work was only cover for one or two days a week and this would take the pressure off me and would give me chance to recover from the stress-related headaches. Not a moment too soon or a moment too late our future had been taken care of and we were so grateful to the Lord.

The next step was the wedding arrangements and the difficult task of doing the best we could on our individual meagre resources. But even in those matters God was at work and, by His grace, was entering into and sorting them out for us. One of the staff members at Moorlands regularly used a local taxi firm and knew them well. She persuaded them to do our wedding taxis at a discounted rate! The organist at the Methodist Church I attended in Whitby town centre gave his services for free. Rev'd Ernest Willis, our Minister, also gave his services for free, and also arranged for us to have free use of a beautiful large downstairs room in the Chapel building for our wedding reception. This was a beautiful room with stained glass windows with flowers of the Bible all along one wall. As a 'thank you' for taking on the extra responsibilities whilst the Manageress was away in hospital I had been given a considerable bonus from Methodist Guild Holidays on top of my usual salary, and this was exactly the right amount of money needed to pay for all the wedding flowers. A lady at Church kindly offered to arrange those in the Church and the Reception Room for free. My dear friend Kathleen, the cook, graciously offered to make and decorate the 3 tier wedding cake, and Margaret, her assistant cook and also my friend, agreed to do all the catering for the reception at a really inexpensive cost. Kathleen also undertook to help me find suitable material for the bridesmaid dresses, to go with my wedding dress, and to find an appropriate pattern. Julie, on staff for a year before going to University, and a keen photographer, offered to do the photography. It couldn't have worked out better, and every single aspect of the wedding was taken care of, and within those meagre financial means of Denis and myself. Several dear friends of Moorlands even offered their help in other ways, such as coming on the morning of the wedding to help prepare the rooms for the incoming holiday guests so that those staff invited to and/or involved in the wedding could have the time off.

Everything that all of these wonderful friends did was absolutely 'top-notch' and Denis and I felt privileged to have them as our friends. The Lord had worked through the kindness and the generosity of these people to provide for **all** our needs, and we wanted for nothing.

CHAPTER FOURTEEN

ANOTHER NEW BEGINNING

'I Virginia, take thee Denis…for my lawful wedded husband…for better for worse, for richer for poorer, in sickness and in health'

(The marriage Service)

The wedding day dawned, and as I awoke, instead of feeling indescribable joy – as I should – I felt absolutely dreadful! For a week I had been struggling with a virus which the doctor had assured me would be cleared by our wedding day. As I lay there in bed – my wedding day – I wondered how on earth I would cope. 'Lord please help me through this day' I prayed 'and help me to be well and enjoy it as I should, and not to spoil it for Denis and everyone else'. After that I had little time for thinking about how I felt as the day became very busy, but as I went through the motions of attending the hairdresser, getting changed with my four bridesmaids, and greeting my dear Mother-in-Christ Irene, Denis's best man Inderjit, and all four bridesmaids, I still felt pretty 'groggy'.

Time drew near and the taxis arrived and took Denis and his best man to the Church, followed by the bridesmaids. Despite my very definite attempts to be at the Church on time, and to defy people's silly superstitions on these matters, 5-10 minutes later than arranged the taxi arrived for Irene and I. As we set off for the Church, which was only 10 minutes drive away, I suddenly felt on top again and the viral symptoms which had dogged me for over a week completely disappeared. When we arrived at the Church and stepped out of the taxi I was met with 4 visions of loveliness all grouped on the Church steps. These were my bridesmaids – Denis's sister Rose and her daughter Joann; a friend's daughter Judith; and my friend Kathleen who was my chief bridesmaid.

Back, left to right: Joann, Rose. Front, left to right: Kathleen, Judith

My heart lifted as I was about to step into this completely new phase of my life surrounded by friends who had meant so much to me and those who were to become my new family. I was flooded with the peace and joy of knowing that again I was in the right place at the right time, and completely within the will of God. As the music started up it was such a joy to be walking down the aisle of the Church on the arm of my Mother-in-Christ, surrounded and supported on all sides by friends given me by Christ, and walking towards the man Christ had given me to be my husband. Standing at the front Denis and his best man were outnumbered as six females walked down the aisle of the Church towards them!

Then another amazing thing happened. The very large Church was about half full, but with people dotted about the pews. However as the organ struck up for the first hymn the sound of singing far exceeded the number of voices and people within that congregation. There was such a crescendo of singing as if the Church was full to overflowing! This was a very unusual experience and hard to comprehend but I felt that heaven was rejoicing at the union of Denis and I, and that those witnesses who had gone on before us into heaven were joining with us and rejoicing with us – swelling the chorus. It was the most tremendous experience. As we sang the hymn whose words had been part of God's guidance to join our lives, my mind flashed back to the fuller meaning of those words and the memories they now evoked. The last verse of the hymn had special meaning to me:

> And if our fellowship below
> In Jesus be so sweet,
> What heights of rapture shall we know
> When round His throne we meet!

Firstly I was reminded of that lovely time in the Methodist church at Hawksworth, and the rapturous fellowship enjoyed as people came and went and joined in fellowship, singing round the organ. Then there were those poignant Friday evenings at 'Moorlands' when, before the guests and staff parted company the following day we would walk across the road from Moorlands to the cliff-top overlooking the sea, stand in a large circle with hands tightly clasped and sing that last verse together. Those were wonderful but poignant moments, often looking out at a wonderful sunset over the sea, but often with a lump in our throats and tears in our eyes. Now, in this church, at this wedding ceremony, this verse – the whole hymn – took on a new meaning and a new significance.

It was a wonderful service with many people taking part. My young friend Joanne and her boyfriend Phillip, along with husband and wife friends Paul and June, played and sang modern worship songs during the signing of the Register. In the vestry we could hear the congregation joining in heartily. During the service Michael sang the most beautiful rendering of the Lord's Prayer, music he had written himself. The service led by our Minister, Revd Ernest Willis, was most encouraging for a couple who were about to step out into the unknown future together with very little by way of the finances or possessions and not quite knowing what the future held. He preached from the passage Luke 12: 22-31.

The rest of the day was a bit of a haze, as it often is on such happy and busy occasions, but it was wonderful to be surrounded by so many Christian friends. We had our wedding photographs taken in the Park close by to the church – a beautiful setting.

I was introduced to many of Denis's relations and friends whom I had never met, and it was hard to remember who was who! My dear Mother-in-Christ, Irene, gave the speech usually given by the Bride's Father, and I felt my day was complete and perfect. At the reception I was surprised and delighted to find that Edith from Moorlands had made four small cakes and dressed them in the material from which my bridesmaids dresses were made.

Wedding cake made by Kathleen and bridesmaid cakes by Edith

They were beautiful. Edith had learnt to do these at a local evening class many years ago but we have been unable to find out whether this was a local tradition. After a long but very happy reception we were finally whisked back to Moorlands to change for our honeymoon and, amidst the usual goodbyes and the decorating of the car, we drove off to start the rest of our life together.

It was at that point that the virus started to kick in again and I felt pretty dreadful as we drove off from Whitby to our destination in Cumbria where we were to honeymoon. This was followed by our first night on honeymoon during which I had very bad breathing difficulties. This resulted in a mad dash the following day to hospital in Kendal where a lung infection was diagnosed. The Lord had certainly ensured that the infection I had did not mar the happiest day of my life, whatever happened after it. Praise Him!

CHAPTER FIFTEEN

DECISION TIME

'He makes me to lie down in fresh, tender green pastures: He leads me beside the still and restful waters' (Psalm 23 : 2 Amp)

THE HONEYMOON WAS over and it was the start of an unknown future. However, not quite so unknown due to going back to a new job with a former employer. There was excitement at again seeing those old friends at Green Park, the elderly Jewish folk I looked after in my former job as full-time Warden. The excitement was tinged with great sadness that in the 3 years since I had left to go to Whitby some of those dearly loved old folk had passed away. However there was the anticipation of sharing my life with Denis and the sharing together of our Christian faith, and this took the edge off some of the sadness I experienced at never seeing again those dear friends.

It wasn't long before we had settled into our flat on site, and we were grateful for all that it gave to us for this new start in our lives together. Our furniture was spartan but we had all that was necessary, and much of that had been provided yet again through others. The lovely drop leaf table with its barley twist legs (later thought to be an antique) and a set of four dining chairs had been given to us by Revd Kathleen Bowe, a kindly female Tutor from Cliff College. Two lovely old and very comfortable chairs had been given by a Christian aunt and uncle of Denis. From wedding present money kindly given us by several people we managed to afford a new bed and also one or two cheap carpet squares. By the world's standards we hadn't much but it was enough to get us started and until we got on our feet financially, and we recognized the Lord's gracious provision for us through the gracious giving of others. For a week or two (was that all?) we enjoyed much time together in this new part-time job of mine, and as Denis started to sign on for work.

Then out of the blue the full-time Warden took sick and I suddenly found myself covering full-time for one development, and part-time for the other development across the road! Life suddenly became very over-busy again. Wasn't this why I had left here in the first place? Although it was hectic, with the extra help given me by Denis it was not as cumbersome as previous. The hardest part of all was when I had to go across to the other development and sleep overnight on a sofa bed in what was normally used as an office. If the weather was wet I found myself walking into a cold office with a wet floor onto which I had to let down the sofa-bed provided. Not exactly ideal conditions for sleeping on. Denis agreed to come across and sleep there with me, which I appreciated. Eventually the employers kindly fitted a bed onto the wall which dropped down onto legs, so not actually onto the cold, wet floor! They eventually also provided a large carpet square.

It was a strange time, one when although Denis was trying to find work we were not too clear whether we were meant to stay in Leeds or not. Work was not easy to find despite Denis's many attempts at being willing to do anything. Even though our Christian friends at the local church kept their eyes and ears open and passed on details of anything they heard about, none of these were forthcoming with a work offer.

Eventually we wondered if we were meant to use this time back at Green Park as a 'staging post' – a transitional period. So Denis started to look at jobs advertised further afield. The difficulty was that we were still restricted in that we were unable to look at anything unless it had a home to go with it. This narrowed the field considerably and we began to wonder where God's will was in all of this. We weren't really settled in the Sheltered Housing complex but we were most grateful for what it provided for the time being.

Again came another verse from Mum Irene; this must have been towards the end of the time I had a back injury, which had meant staying flat on my back for weeks. During this time Denis was avidly looking for work and the poem reflects this:

> Oh, Ginny dear, I'm truly sad.
> To hear your back is aching bad.
> And that you have to lie in bed.
> With thoughts a-buzzing in your head.
>
> But, stay a moment – what a blessing
> You have dear Denis, kind, caressing,
> Cherishing and full of care
> To guard you from too great despair.

I hear you have a busy week
So to get well I know you'll seek,
And so I trust when comes this letter,
Virginia is feeling better.
And that you both by then will be
Able your family to see.

I pray and trust your way comes clear
And God's direction you will hear;
So quietly wait, with patience too,
Till He reveal what you must do.
He is beside you, changes not,
And for you both His plan He's got.
I pray His Hand will open wide
And in His pleasure you'll abide.

Denis applied for a job in Folkestone, the work of which was rather vaguely advertised and which implied there may be a partner aspect to it. He got an interview which we were both required to attend and felt that at least we would receive clarification about the partner aspect. The people who interviewed were lovely but there was some uncertainty about the terms and conditions of employment, which were not made clear. It seemed they were trying to get out of paying proper National Insurance contributions by employing me rather than Denis, yet it was Denis who had applied for the job, been accepted for the interview, and wanted to do the work. This troubled us, particularly with relation to national insurance contributions and future pension implications. Then we found out that our staff living accommodation was split and the rooms were far apart from each other with communal areas between them and we felt this was totally unsuitable for us as a newly married couple. We returned home very dejected and unsure whether this was right. After much prayerful consideration we felt it was not. Notification was received that someone else had been appointed so that seemed to confirm our thinking, and to clarify our ethical concerns on this matter. However some time later we received a telephone call to say that the person appointed had left and would we take up the post. We tried to kindly explain that after much thought we had come to the conclusion it wasn't right for us but the person at the other end of the telephone line wasn't taking this very kindly and insisted we explain fully why not. We started to do so but as we did the telephone connection was cut. We tried repeatedly, over many hours, to ring back and carry on the conversation but to no avail, and they never got back to us. We took that as confirmation that we were never meant to go to that place.

A while later there were two jobs advertised which Denis applied for. One of them was a job with the Billy Graham Association in England. The only trouble was that it didn't mention accommodation. However we decided that we would write and explain our predicament about housing and ask if they would be providing accommodation with the job.

At the same time a job for a Church caretaker in Derbyshire was advertised and this had accommodation to go with the job. Denis decided to apply for that, especially as he had been doing the job of a Janitor at the College, which equipped him fully for this work. When he got an interview with them we had still not heard from the Billy Graham organisation, but we didn't expect that the caretaker's job in the church would make an immediate decision on who to appoint, so there would be opportunity to weigh up the two options when and if we heard from Billy Graham's organisation.

The Church was a lovely one, had been fully refurbished inside, and it was obvious it had a lot of activities going on. There were several couples attending the interview and it was a bit daunting to be sat waiting with other people, all vying for the same job! Denis's interview went well and, to our surprise, he was very quickly offered and accepted the job. Ah well, Billy Graham hadn't replied so perhaps that wasn't meant to be. Just after Denis had accepted the job, and it was too late to back out, they did reply and asked us to go down for an interview and said they would probably be able to help us with housing. Whilst it would seem that circumstances and the Lord decided for us, I have often wondered since what would have happened had we been able to go for that other interview, whether Denis would have got the job, and if we would have been happy there. I had longed to be involved with the Billy Graham organisation, having made a partial commitment to Christ at one of his crusade meetings. But circumstances dictated differently, and there had to be no looking back.

And so we moved into the new job with home and Denis started this new full time job. It was good for him to be employed full time again, and in Christian service, and for a short while we were very happy. We made several friends in the church but it wasn't long before we found that we were very much tied to the place and able to get out very little if at all. Denis had to work during the day and then be on duty at night to open up for groups using the church. This meant being around in case they had any problems, and being there to clear up after them and lock up late at night. We hardly ever left the premises, and began to feel like prisoners. Even Denis's preaching appointments were difficult to fulfil as they took him outside this church and into others further afield, and this made for conflicts with the requirements of his employers.

Then things went from bad to worse as Denis started to suffer with asthma. This was something he had never suffered before, although it did run in his family and his mother had suffered with asthma quite badly most of her life. There were many trips to the local doctor, and although he was sympathetic, Denis only got the very barest medical help via a Ventolin inhaler – a simple reliever for the actual symptoms. As a result of him being constantly out of breath and tight-chested his work slowed down because he felt so ill. From this point on he received no sympathy or help from the church officials at all. They tried to make out that he was deliberately slacking in his work, and even warned him about it – verbally and in writing. This was unbelievable and we were absolutely devastated. Here was a man who prided himself in his work and who took great delight in doing it well, despite its menial aspect, and who had received glowing references from Cliff College in that respect. Yet in this Christian Church they would not admit that here was a man with a medical problem which was not his fault. Eventually, in desperation, Denis sought a note from his doctor which explained the difficulties but even then, for some strange reason we will never understand, they refused to believe that he was not deliberately slacking in his job. They continued to formally (verbally and in writing) berate him about this.

What on earth could we do? Denis was getting more and more ill and I was becoming more and more distraught. The illness I had suffered while in Whitby, and which had disappeared for a while, now returned due to the stress, and between us we struggled to cope with life. So I started to pray that the Lord would show us a way out. It is very important that I relate here that despite being treated like this by Christians I had not turned against God, nor the Christian Church. The Lord had matured me enough to help me realise that this was not His doing but that of certain misguided people. It is important that when things go wrong in life we do not blame God. He has only the very best in store for us (as my following chapters will reveal) but when He created He gave His people free will, and some of them, even those who claim to belong to Him, don't always behave as He would have them do. That is not God's fault, but theirs, and we have to be careful not to lay the blame for their actions and words at His feet. It has been my experience that whatever life or people throw at us, God has always used the circumstances to bring something good out of them. I continue to be amazed at how He does this and what good fruit He can bear from the most unfortunate of situations. What happened next is an example of this.

At the back of our flat in the Church building were industrial buildings, with high railing between us and them. One day, as I prayed about the problems surrounding Denis's health and his job of work, the sign of a cross appeared. As I watched the cross rose from below the railings that divided our flat from the rest of society around us, and it went up and over the railings, as it were 'on the outside' of what now felt like our prison and the prison bars. It stayed there for some time. I realised that this was the way in which the sun had taken hold of something and made the figure of a cross appear and that it was the steady moving of the sun which took it into that final position. However, despite my logical thinking on this matter the most tremendous sense of peace suddenly swept over me. I felt that God had given me a sign; that He was telling me He was in charge of this situation and would get us out of what had become to feel like a prison. Again came one of Mum's poems:

Keep on keeping on
However rough the way,
Just hold His hand
And understand
He asks you to obey.
At times we find it hard to know,
The path that He has planned,
But He will make it clearly known
And we *shall* understand.

So, keep on keeping on,
Sufficient is His care
And more sufficient is His love
So, why should we despair?

Little was I to realise just how gracious He would be in his dealings with us, nor how wonderfully He would take charge of this situation. As mum had written he would indeed hold our hands during the difficult time and He would make His path clearly known to us in ways we could not have envisaged.

CHAPTER SIXTEEN

RELEASE!

'My chains fell off, my heart was free' (Hymns & Psalms 216)

HOLIDAYS WERE FEW, and those we had were taken in very cheap self-catering properties. In early 1988 we booked a holiday for later that year. We did so early in order that someone didn't get that particular cheap accommodation before us! Where holidays are concerned, and the cost of them, this has always been the way we have had to work. We had booked the caravan in Cumbria where we had gone for our honeymoon. The caravan was owned by Christian farmers who had been very kind to us, and due to the difficult situation we were in we were particularly looking forward to this holiday in July. However about one or two weeks before we were due to go we received a telephone call to apologise that they had double booked the caravan and that the people who had booked it first were the other couple. We were so deflated and so devastated. We so desperately needed to get away from the Church and the situation, and to where the air would be purer and free from the pollution which was damaging Denis's health.

What could we do? Then we had an idea. Our friend Mike and Val had a caravan, and we wondered if they would be kind enough to allow us to use it for the two weeks we had set aside for Denis's holiday from work, and if so to ask if they would tow it to a place of our choice for a holiday. We rang. Yes, of course they would! "Where would you like to go?" asked Mike. We thought carefully and realised that our holiday coincided with Derwent Convention Week at Cliff College and we were now in Derbyshire so not too far to travel. What a wonderful opportunity to attend and get not only the refreshment we needed for our health and well being but also spiritual refreshment as well. Mike was only too pleased to bring the caravan over, and so it was organised. Little did we know that this was to be the beginning of a wonderful period in our married life.

The week of Derwent Convention was dreadful. It poured with rain almost all week. We walked from the caravan site each day in our heavy weather gear and boots and sat dripping in the tent meetings, trying hard to get warm. July? This was more like autumn or winter. However despite the weather the spiritual uplift was wonderful and we enjoyed every minute of every day.

During Derwent Week I had an interview for a job in Leeds. Due to Denis's continuing failing health, and in desperation to try and get out of what was becoming an impossible work/home situation, we agreed that if Denis couldn't work to support us then I would. Because of my experience as a Sheltered Housing Warden I had applied for and received an interview for similar work with a Christian organisation in Leeds. The interview was in the middle of the first week of our holidays. So off we went to Leeds for my interview.

It was a good interview, and the people were nice, but then came the very searching questions, some of which caused me to think very carefully about what they were asking and expecting of their new member of staff. It became clear that in the Lounge where residents would congregate several social pursuits would be taking place which would be the job of the appointed person to organise and carry out. One of these would be Bingo. I thought very carefully and then stated that I did not believe in gambling and that I could not be a party to organising and carrying out activities such as Bingo. In view of my knowledge of this organisation I was very surprised that they would even think about promoting such activities. I knew as soon as I said it that I had blown any chances of being offered the job, and ensuing questions to me on issues on which they and I did not agree or see eye to eye just confirmed that this was not right for me.

On our drive back to Cliff College I felt dreadful and did an awful lot of apologising to Denis that I had blown any chance of getting a job which could have got us out of a situation which was not helping his health. He was most understanding and agreed that we had to stick to our principles in life. In the days that followed we were helped much on this issue. As we shared the story of the interview with others they assured me that I had done the right thing. This was most gratifying and I began to feel much better about it. I had to constantly remind myself that all of this was in God's hands and that He knew what He was about. I also remembered the cross which arose above and beyond the railings which separated us from our home and job in the church and from the rest of the world, and continued to believe it was His promise to me.

Then one day the person leading the Bible Studies expounded on the passage which contained these words, 'do not conform to the standards of the world, but be transformed by Christ.' From that point on I felt God was really telling me that I had done the right thing in not conforming to those things that the world thought nothing of but which I felt were wrong, and that He really was in charge of our whole situation. We were very soon to find out!

Mum wrote this:

> We cannot look ahead and see!
> But we can trust, take heart and say
> "I'll trust the Lord to guide my way"
> In pastures new, mountain or vale
> He'll lead you on, He will not fail,
> And as in faith you kneel and pray,
> His star will guide you on your way.

During that first week we bumped into Sharon, the Principal's Secretary and a very good friend and former work colleague of Denis. "Denis" she said "are you going to apply for your old job?". Denis, nonplussed, asked what she was talking about. It transpired that the young man who had taken over from Denis as Janitor when he left to marry me was now talking of leaving. This was a strange and very remarkable situation. The reason for this is that during our first holiday after we were married Denis had a very clear and unforgettable dream which he related to me at that time. The dream was about Cliff College. The dream was lengthy but even the morning after, and for a long time to come, its details remained very clear to Denis. In it Edna, the Matron, was absolutely bowed down by work and wondering how on earth she could cope. There was a lot more to the dream and he had related all of it to me. At that time I had felt led to say to Denis "If you got the opportunity to go back to Cliff College to work would you do so?" I remember being surprised at his reply, particularly as we had both felt quite clearly at the time we left our respective jobs that we had made the right decision. "Yes" said Denis "I think I would." We both realised, though, that the accommodation aspect would have to be different to that which was originally provided. At the time of the dream we never thought there would ever be opportunity for another job at Cliff, but I must admit that I never forget that dream of his nor the clarity of the happenings within it; it never quite strayed from the back of my mind. Now, at this moment in time, that dream came flooding back to both of us quite vividly.

During that week there was not opportunity to enquire further about this possible job opportunity as all the staff and Dr Davies the Principal were heavily involved in the Convention. But surprisingly when Denis bumped into Edna during that week she was indeed very heavily overburdened by her work. This was a surprise as she was an extremely capable lady who usually rose above all that life and work threw at her. In relating to us how she felt and what was happening, the full details of that dream came flooding back again as they mirrored exactly what she was now saying to us. We both began to feel that God was speaking to us about the forthcoming vacancy of Denis's former job.

During the second week of our holiday, when Derwent Convention had finished, Denis managed to obtain an interview with Dr Davies, the Principal of the College, at which time he enquired about the possibility of his old job becoming vacant again. The situation was complicated due to the work which Denis's predecessor was hoping to go to, but it did appear that there would be a vacancy in the very near future. Dr Davies said he would be delighted to have Denis back in the job, but said "you must realise Denis that we are obliged to advertise the vacancy and you would have to take your chance with other applicants". That was fair enough and we rested content that if it was God's will it would indeed happen. If it wasn't then He would find us another way out of our difficulties.

From the end of July until mid November there were anxious times as we continued in the church situation, and as Denis's asthma returned after the holiday. He struggled on and despite the difficulties encountered with his employers we tried to keep our hopes and our spirits up. Eventually we had a telephone call from Maurice, the College Administrator. "Denis" he said, "your predecessor is leaving suddenly and we are now in a situation where we are unable to advertise the post as we need to fill it as quickly as possible. If you are still interested we must at the least interview you." Of course we agreed! An interview for both of us was arranged quickly, and we upped our prayers for guidance for all of us in this matter.

The day dawned and although we were both convinced that this had worked out so miraculously because it was meant to be and was the answer to our prayers, nevertheless there were knots in both our stomachs as we arrived at the College for the interview. It went well, although it was extremely searching. Finally we were asked what kind of commitment we would be willing to make to the job if Denis were appointed. Before we had time to consider Denis replied "at least 5 years." I had secretly and quickly thought much of a much longer time period, but I realised that in offering at least 5 years Denis was offering far more than previous Janitors for several years had given. This lack of commitment to the job had in fact proved problematical to the College, as I had learnt from Denis when he recounted his experience of taking over the job in 1983. In less than a week we had a formal letter from Maurice informing us that Denis had got the job and asking how soon he could start and we could move in! What a wonderful answer to prayer and in what an amazing way God had worked!

CHAPTER SEVENTEEN

TIMES OF REFRESHING

'I came that they may have and enjoy life, and have it in abundance, to the full, till it overflows' (John 10 : 10 Amp)

DENIS COMPLETED HIS work at the church and we moved into Cliff College during the last week in November 1988. Our home was to be the flatlet containing a lovely large first floor room located above the Administration Office and the College entrance, the room where Denis had formerly lived when he worked there three years before. The room was surrounded on three sides with long old- fashioned sash windows, almost floor to ceiling. It had views down the lane from the College onto the main road, and glorious views across the College orchard and beyond it to the hills known as Curbar Gap and Baslow Edge – a local beauty spot for tourists and walkers. On the third side our windows looked across to the Principals first floor house and to the kitchen yard below. We had also been given an additional room on the same floor but located outside of our flat and along a corridor, to use as our bedroom.

The flat consisted of the large room, a tiny kitchenette, a bathroom larger than the kitchen (!) and a separate toilet. The Flat was a curious shape and dimension but had originally been the College Sanatorium, so its usage wasn't exactly designed as a home for two and all that entailed. The kitchen was a problem in that it was so narrow we could not even stretch our arms out sideways full length. There were no kitchen units of any kind and only a small old-fashioned sink underneath the window which overlooked the lane. As a relatively new married couple we had opted to do our own catering and live our own life in the flat rather than take all our meals in the College with the students. Due to the stress illness I didn't think I could cope with intense communal living. I could not cope with a lot of noise or talking or listening, all of which brought on the headaches. Also as a fairly new married couple we felt that we still needed a modicum of privacy. However in making that decision to live independently in our flat how on earth would we be able to cater for ourselves with such inadequate facilities?

To our rescue came Bill, a beaming Christian and a joiner by trade – helping out at that time at the College, although not actually employed there full time. He offered to help. We bought some inexpensive kitchen units from MFI and he chopped them down to size and fitted them into the narrow kitchen and also into the corridor outside the kitchen. The latter became an overflow storage section of our small kitchen. We then bought ourselves a small tabletop cooker which had a tiny oven with two rings on top of it, and we were set to go! Many years later, and looking back, I cannot now imagine how on earth we managed to cook on such inadequate facilities. But we did and I even managed to prepare dinner parties for between four and six – our friends and us – on that cooker!

So life began at Cliff College, that place I had heard such a lot about, especially in my younger days as a teenager when, as I have recounted earlier, Irene used to take some of the young folk to Cliff at the special times of the College year. I could hardly believe that I was now living in the place I had heard such a lot about, the place where Irene and Joe had such happy times there with others; the place where Irene's sister Ethelwynne had met her husband Joe and, under God's direction, had married him and gone to America where Joe had become part of the Billy Graham organisation.

These and many other exciting stories had been recounted to me about Cliff College and the people who had been involved with its work in the past, and here I was! As time went by I was to learn much more of these people as Denis was more steeped in Cliff College and its history than I realised, and over the years he had met many people whom Irene had told me about. As a mother-in-Christ, and a Christ-given husband, Denis and Irene had more in common with each other than I think they realised. How wise was God in His choice of my friends and my husband, and how wonderful when He brought together their interests and connections. Amazing!

Living in the flat, although it had certain restrictions and difficulties, was a great joy. The large room was wonderful for entertaining our friends. Blue tits and other beautiful birds with colourful plumage came frequently to eat from the bird feeders outside our large windows; and much time was spent watching the squirrels dashing up and down the trees just across the road – trees whose tops we could see well from this vantage point on the first floor. Apart from the occasional noises from the lane below us, and the banging of the College entrance door immediately below the flat when the students came in late at night, many quiet and tranquil times were spent gazing down the College orchard; up and across to the ridge known as Curbar Gap; and watching folk relaxing or quietly praying singly or together in the College orchard. It was one of those places where no-one could pass by without us being able to see them out of our windows, so we hardly ever missed seeing friends or acquaintances if they happened to visit the College!

Life was good. Of course life was busy for Denis, but he had good colleagues in different College departments and there was a very close bond between them. During that first year his friends from his earlier job at Cliff were still working there and it was good for him to renew those close friendships, and for me to forge links with them too. During our time there links were forged with some that would last a long time. Sharon, the Principal's Secretary, and a good friend of Denis, would continue as a good friend to both of us for many years to come, even when she moved around the country after being ordained as a Methodist Minister. Edna, the College Matron and Denis's immediate Head of Department, was a great blessing during our first year there and until her retirement a year later. Our friendship with her has continued across intervening years, especially due to the involvement we have with the local Bible Society Action Group of which we and she are still members. Edna was a very wise lady and deeply spiritual, and one could always depend on her for wise counsel and prayer support. Friends like that are absolute gems in our walk with Christ and to this day we still value those Christ-like qualities in our friendship with her and others. June worked on the domestic team and so her work brought her into close contact with Denis. When she finally retired from her work at Cliff we became firm friends and did our weekly shopping together, during which we talked 'Cliff College' matters quite a lot and also put Cliff College and the world to rights many times!

**June at retirement party (middle of back row)
with other staff and family members**

Although life was busy for Denis the camaraderie with staff members, the times of good fellowship, and the gratification of doing a job well and being appreciated for it, helped to make up for the long hours and the hard work. All in all we felt we were at the place we were meant to be for the time being, although had no idea that we would be there far longer than the five years Denis had envisaged.

That first year was wonderful. I did not work at first and I spent many happy hours going to join Denis and the staff at their morning coffee and afternoon tea breaks. There was banter, and teasing, and happy fellowship at these times, as one would expect from a Christian group all gelling together. If the weather was good and if Sharon wasn't too busy to take her coffee breaks, then several of us would end up taking our drinks outside, sitting on the seat on the Principal's lawn. Sharon was well-known for sunbathing and took every opportunity to soak it up! Years later, when visiting her at various Methodist manses, one would find she hadn't changed. Copious mugs of tea taken outside on sun loungers was still the order of the day!

Life continued at a steady space, until one day...

CHAPTER EIGHTEEN

USEFUL FOR GOD

' God has appointed. . . those with gifts of administration'

(1 Corinthians 12 : 28)

I HAD NOT been looking for a job of work. My 'tension headaches' had continued, despite praying for healing, and I didn't feel I could cope with work amongst other people and the stress that seemed to arise from being constantly around them and with ongoing conversations etc. These things seemed to exacerbate the headaches. Although weren't exactly well-off by the world's standards we had no rent or council tax to pay, and even our electricity was paid for by the College, so it seemed we could manage without a second wage.

However one day as I wandered down to the village post office I noted a postcard in its window. It read something like 'Stoney Middleton Parish Council requires a part-time Parish Clerk'. My attention was particularly drawn by the Parish Council bit of the advert. Many years before I had been a Councillor on a Town Council in West Yorkshire, a community role I had enjoyed immensely, and I had much admired the work undertaken by Jackie, the assistant Town Clerk. When I saw the advert I felt that it would be interesting to tackle Parish Council work from the opposite end – being the Clerk (the administrator) rather than the Councillor.

After prayerful consideration I decided to apply. It was only part-time so I felt that I could perhaps cope with a few hours a week. I also felt that all I had done in recent years had well equipped me for such work. As recounted earlier I had held many jobs where I had run offices, written business letters, helped work out quotations, dealt with simple accounts, and been in charge of organisations of various kinds. Although I didn't have paper qualifications, and wasn't absolutely sure I was meant to be working, I prayed about it, applied, and left it to the Lord to show me if it was right or not. I was telephoned a few days later by the existing Clerk, who was leaving the job due to moving away from the area. She arranged a date and time for me to have the interview and, due to the lack of good transport links, even arranged to pick me up in her car and take me there. It transpired from conversation with her that there were three of us to attend for interview that night.

I duly arrived at the school where interviews were taking place and one of the Councillors came out and asked if I would mind waiting as the person to be interviewed before me hadn't yet turned up. Quite some time passed during which I heard the interviewing panel chatting and laughing in another classroom. No-one else arrived. Eventually I was asked to go through and apologies were made that I had been kept waiting. Fortunately I had a really good reference from

Marjorie Brown of Moorlands at Whitby. She had given me this before I left my job there and told me I could use it if and when I ever needed to apply for another job. She had kindly written glowingly of my office and managerial skills, and my organisational skills as a social secretary. After a very brief interview I was asked to wait in another classroom while the councillors discussed me. I didn't expect to be told there and then, especially as there was at least one other person to interview. However I was soon called back into the room and told that in view of my obvious abilities they would like me to take the job if I would be willing.

I was overwhelmed! I had expected they would wish to consider the other two applicants first and, despite my glowing reference from Marjorie, I guess I thought too much about my lack of 'proper qualifications'. I was only too happy to accept the job especially when I learnt that apart from the actual Council Meetings I would be working from home on my own. This meant that I could to fit the work in as I could cope with it and at my own pace, avoiding the pressure which brought on the dreaded headaches. This was a wonderful answer to prayer and I did, of course, accept the job as I felt that all had transpired to lead me to it. I later found out that the person who should have been interviewed before me had turned up after I had been offered the job; I never heard what happened to the third applicant.

Thus began 15 years of the most interesting work, and contact with people from varied professions, local authorities and other organisations. As time went by I had no doubt that, although this work was not in a Christian environment as some of my other jobs had been, God does lead His children into secular situations for His purposes and for us to be His witness in the wider world and to help others in many different ways.

My role was multi-faceted. In the beginning my official title in Law was 'The Proper Officer of the Council'. In later years it was to become that plus 'The Responsible Financial Officer'. I was a minute-taker for Council meetings; a secretary for dealing with outgoing and incoming correspondence and telephone calls; the person who had to ensure that all Council dealings kept to the letter of the Law (very legalistic and quite cumbersome); along with lots of other minor aspects of the work.

It was in dealing with the legal side of things that it seemed to me the work for God came into play. How easy it is for us Christians to assume that God only works through us in a preaching or an evangelistic role. He does in fact use us in all kinds of ways and in all kinds of situations, and we mustn't tie Him down to our own expectations of how He can do that. The legalistic aspect of my role required me to understand the reasons why some things had to be done in a certain way. I then needed to be able to explain this to them in a way which did not offend them but helped them to understand the moral and ethical aspects to their very important volunteer work. This was work they were undertaking on behalf of their community, and the community at large did not always understand how hard and complicated it could be for them.

For me to do this was not easy and I had to learn a lot of patience. I also had to learn to understand where each Councillor was coming from in their attitudes to the laws imposed upon them by Act of Parliament and then be able to gently guide their understanding. As the years went by this became more burdensome for them as the legal requirements upon them both as a Body and as individuals increased greatly. However in all of this I did see that God can use us through our moral and ethical conduct and that this can speak to others every bit as much as the obvious preaching etc.

Those 15 years spent working from home and for the Parish Council was a tremendous learning curve. I got to know many people, all of them most interesting. It was a great privilege to work with and for many different people who took up the work of a Parish Councillor, and to make lasting friendships with one or two whom I greatly respected. There were, as in all situations, difficult times, but as a child of God He never failed to carry me through, often using Councillors and others to encourage me with kindly words. I learnt that God not only works through His own but often through others too.

It would be remiss of me to not mention three persons in particular, whom I held in very high regard. Dave (David) had been a councillor for several years before I ever took on the job and was an extremely capable and wise person. I greatly valued his wisdom and, on rare occasions when there were things troubling me, I also appreciated his very helpful and carefully considered advice. As a Councillor he would often sit and listen very carefully to what was being said and, however difficult the issue being discussed, and however fraught the Councillors became about how to deal with it, Dave would then with great wisdom quietly suggest a way forward.

Another great blessing to me was Joy, who became a councillor about halfway through my time as Parish Clerk. In latter years there were many difficulties for the councillors due to the extra requirements on them from Government legislation and these caused conflict, not only between the councillors but sometimes, sadly, between me and them. I had to be seen to advise them according to the Law, and there was always good reason for that, but this was often extremely cumbersome to them and they would ask why I was pressing them to abide by these requirements. At these times I found a great ally in Joy. As a councillor she had no problem in understanding what the Law required of her as an individual, nor why it had to be carried out in a certain way. When I was pressed on all sides by those who disagreed and seemed to blame me for something not of my own making, Joy was always there with words of comfort, support, and encouragement. I felt that unknown to her, who never confessed a faith in Christ, she was a blessing brought to me by the Lord to help in times of trouble. We became firm friends and she was good to work with. I acknowledge her for her integrity, which was beyond reproach and second to none.

The third person was Jack. He had lived in the village for all or most of his life and his knowledge about people and the history of the village was invaluable. If ever the history of a situation needed exploring Jack was readily available to talk to me on the phone or to allow me to talk to him at home. These people were invaluable assets to their community and to me as their servant.

In the normal 'run of the mill' every day, much of my work involved contact with The Peak District National Park Authority, where we were situated. It is a very beautiful area, and attracts many tourists whose presence boosts the economy tremendously. However there are inevitably tensions in this. One of the issues often coming before the Parish Council was affordable housing. Little did I know that as I sat and listened to discussions on the lack of housing for local people, particularly young couples, I would be led in later years to deal with this at a much deeper level. Unknown to me this was a preparation for the future.

Peak Park also made grants for specific projects that

would enhance the countryside and much of my time was spent investigating these, thereby saving paying for local amenities or improvements from council-tax payers money. It was a great thrill to chase up and actually find grants for specific projects, and it reminded me of my days in Youth Club work when I was seeking money to help the Club keep going because local authority funds ran out. There is a certain thrill in being able to raise money for good causes, and it is always less embarrassing and easier than trying to obtain it for oneself.

So this work went on year by year. Month by month I drove from Cliff College to Stoney Middleton, about 2 miles away, dreading the winter. The Council met in the local Junior and Infants School which was up a very steep hill – probably 1 in 4. I have a morbid fear of snow and ice, a phobia would best describe it. I dread walking in snow and even more dread driving in it. The thought of having to drive or walk up and down that very steep hill in winter filled me with irrational and gripping fear. My stomach would go into knots, my mouth would go dry, and the palms of my hands would go sweaty. Yet in all those years I never need fear. I repeatedly prayed to the Lord about this irrationality and He never failed to help me keep my commitment to the Council. In all of those 15 years it hardly snowed and when it did the answers to my fears came in different ways. My husband Denis, despite needing to have a meal and a rest after a very hard working day, would forgo those, put on his wellington boots, and carry my heavy pilot case with all the Council stuff in, walking me either from Cliff College to the village and up the hill, or from the main road where he had managed to park, and then up the hill. Then he would sit quietly through the meeting, to help me down the steep and slippery hill and home again.

The other answer to prayer was Kath (Kathleen). She started to attend our meetings when she was elected as a Parish Representative to the Peak Park Authority. She was extremely faithful and tried to attend all of the Parish Council meetings within the area she was elected to represent. Kath was a wonderful Christian and it wasn't long before we became good friends. As she had to virtually pass my door on the way to our Council Meeting she started to pick me up in her car. Here also the winter months became less worrying to me as I didn't have the dread of driving up that steep hill. The other bonus was the lovely conversations of faith we had on the journey there and back.

For the most part my time as Parish Clerk was a good and fulfilling time. Stoney Middleton village was a good place with kindly, friendly folk, and I enjoyed getting to know many of them through my work. It was a pleasure to serve not only the Councillors but also the villagers and to feel that I had done my little bit to help improve their lives. I felt very strongly about the advocacy part of my work, and enjoyed promoting the Council to the residents, many of whom did not know just how much Parish Councillors did or what hard work this committed volunteer work was.

However the time came when I felt I had had enough. My stress problem was becoming worse again, no doubt exacerbated by the ever-increasing requirements on the Parish Clerk and also on the Councillors. I was due to retire at 60 in November 2003, but by October of that year I felt so stressed out that I couldn't cope with even hanging on and doing the extra month and so retired after the October Parish Council Meeting. Providentially it was as well that I did.

CHAPTER NINETEEN

ANSWERED PRAYER

'Therefore I tell you, whatever you ask for in prayer, believe that you have received it, and it will be yours' (Mark 11 : 24)

'Do not be anxious about anything, but in everything, by prayer and petition, with thanksgiving, present your requests to God' (Philippians 4 : 6)

'You will call upon me and come and pray to me, I will listen to you' says the Lord' (Jeremiah 29 : 12)

SEVERAL THINGS HAPPENED before, during, and after our time at Cliff, when God said 'yes', 'no' or 'wait' to my prayers. I relate these as they have been part of my growing into Christ, and trusting Him to take care of every part of it. It's wonderful when God says 'yes' unconditionally to our prayers, but sometimes He says 'wait' or 'no'. When the answer is 'no' I have learnt it has been because He had a far wiser plan for me than I could ever imagine. Also that His promises regarding prayer are to be depended upon completely.

Many years ago I read a book by Catherine Marshall, the wife of the great preacher Peter Marshall who went on to become a Minister in the United States of America, and Chaplain to the Senate. Catherine advocated that we keep a prayer diary and I started to do this, with the most amazing results. I came across this diary in our loft as I was writing this book. Here are some of the entries:

- March 1981 onwards – prayed for opportunities to witness to the Lord Jesus Christ or to help people each day and those prayers were answered in abundance.

- July/August 1981 – Prayed about a holiday which was hardly likely to happen because I had little money. I wanted to go to Cornwall but never told a soul about this desire or about my prayers. Then one morning one of my employers asked if I would like to go on holiday to Cornwall with her and the family, all expenses paid!

- July – September 1981 – During my time living with Irene and Joe I had prayed avidly about finding suitable accommodation. Then I was told about a bedsit in a large house just a few miles away. The small wage I had was exactly enough for the rent, electric, food bills, and a little bit over.

- August/September 1981 – prayed about guidance for work with young people and was then asked to temporarily teach the Senior Girls Sunday School class in the Methodist Church. This was a wonderful experience and I was richly blessed by the teenagers.

- December 1981 – In my work with the old people at the Jewish Housing Association I prayed for numerous people. A lady I found difficult to like was always complaining and often had me in tears. After praying about her she changed and became more gentle towards me.

- When the heavy snow came I didn't know how, on my own, I could clear it around the whole Sheltered Housing complex. I prayed prior to going to bed. On waking and looking out of the window a narrow path had been cleared all the way around and out onto the road. I eventually found out that the son of the lady next door had quietly crept up late at night, after it was dark, and cleared it. This was round about the time I had actually prayed.

- An old lady in the complex was terribly confused and I feared she may end up in a mental institution, so prayed about her. She went away for Christmas and came back a changed person, with all confusion gone!

- Christmas Eve 1981 – Snow came again, and I prayed again. On returning from a visit into Leeds I found a gang of teenagers clearing the way yet again.

- February 1982 – One of my old people became very down, suffering with nervous trouble which seemed would go on for ever. He had become a virtual hermit. I prayed for him, and one day shortly after he surprised his wife by getting up early and going into Leeds to do some shopping. When he returned it was as if there had been a complete transformation in him – wouldn't recognize him for the same man. He never looked back from that moment on.

- February 1982 – I had received rather a shock about a personal matter and during that day I wept repeatedly. I then went into Leeds to serve lunches at the Methodist Mission and on the way back I sat quietly on the bus and prayed about the problem. As I did so this verse from the Bible suddenly popped into my mind... 'It shall come to pass that before they call I will answer, and while they are yet speaking I will hear'. I sat on the bus and claimed that promise (something Irene had taught me to do). When I arrived home there was a letter from my Godmother enclosing the following verse:

Trust Him, when darkest thoughts assail thee,
Trust Him, when thy faith is small,
Trust Him, when to simply trust Him
Is the hardest thing of all.

My Godmother had mistakenly dated her letter for that very same day, instead of the day before when she posted it, and it was as if that and the comforting verse were an immediate answer to prayer. I needed that verse to lift me out of my sorrow and upset.

- 3rd April 1982 – I prayed about the daughter of one of my old people, who got very upset with her mother and shouted at her a lot. I prayed to the Lord and asked if He would deal with the daughter in the way He knew best. Later that same day the daughter saw me and said she had listened to the way I spoke to her mother on the intercom system and this had given her a new way of approaching her mother. Thank you Lord for the mysterious but wonderful way in which You work!

- 9/4/82 – One of my old people was in terrible pain in her legs but for some time had refused to go and see a doctor. I prayed quietly that the Lord would heal her in the way He saw best or prompt her to change her mind about the doctor. She told me later that day that she had changed her mind about going to the doctor. In ringing for an appointment she had fully expected that just before the Easter holidays the surgery would be closed, or no appointments available. Despite the fact that the surgery was full with 30 people waiting for appointments the doctor had fitted her in immediately. Praise the Lord!

- 17/4/82 – Had been sat all alone in the kitchen of my flat for two full days, doing my local preaching studies and writing a sermon. I felt so in need of companionship and a little fun and prayed aloud "Oh Lord **please** may I have a bit of fun". One minute later there was a ring at the doorbell. It was my friends, husband and wife Paul and June. They told me they had just been passing by the end of the road and had a sudden urge to call and ask me back to their home for a game of scrabble! I had my bit of fun! 'Your Father knows you need these things'.

- 26/4/82 – First thing that morning I felt the need to pick up my guitar and try to play the winning entry from the Eurovision Song Contest with its lovely words about peace. As I sat writing out the words and the notes I stopped to listen to 'Pause for thought' on Radio 4 where they were referring to Psalm 98 about 'singing a new song to the Lord'. As I did my rounds with the old people one of them told me how she wished she were not so lame so that she could go to the synagogue and sit there and feel the peace. She felt she really needed that. But Synagogue was only open on Saturdays and ladies have to go upstairs, and she couldn't manage stairs. So I prayed that the Lord would help her feel that peace. Oh joy of joys, how wonderfully our Lord answers prayer! All the ladies were stood outside chatting and suddenly someone talked about music, and I happened to mention what I had been doing earlier. They insisted that I brought out my guitar and sing to them. So I did and we all sang the Eurovision contest song about peace. The lady I mentioned above said that had given her the peace she had needed.

- Praying for my mother (Irene), for whom I had some deep concern, I felt led to turn in the Bible to Isaiah 40, verse one, where I read these words 'He will gently lead their mothers...' This was most comforting and I took that as a promise from the Lord and continued to claim His promise to care for my mother in Christ..

- Praying about a member of staff in a place where I worked, and asking for guidance on how to deal with her, I read this... 'Has God given you a leadership role in your organisation? Then pray for wisdom. Remember it's yours for the asking'. I was learning to lean heavily on prayer to the Lord and to seek His word for the answers.

And so to prayers, and amazing answers, during the time at Cliff College. The first thing Denis and I prayed about was our growing discontent with the college accommodation we occupied. The lovely large room above reception, with its lovely views, was great. However the room we used as our bedroom, which was along a corridor from outside our flat, was proving unsuitable in many ways. It was a small area of the college which housed a bedroom for students who were sick and needed to be near to the Matron's accommodation and away from the other students. This corridor had two other bedrooms which were for guests' use and one of these was next to our bedroom. For the most part the rooms along the corridor were fairly quiet but on occasions there was either a student in the sick room needing a lot of attention or having hordes of noisy fellow students visiting, or sometimes a noisy guest next door to us. The entrance door to the corridor was right outside our bedroom and it was a swing door. As a result every time someone passed through at night it banged shut and woke us up with a start. After a while this really began to get to us. Denis had to get up very early for work and the constant waking up from the banging door and students or guests began to take a toll on his health due to lack of sleep. We became so desperate at one time that we even asked if we could live out – try and get the Council to offer us a council property. The answer was categorically 'no' as Denis was meant to live on the job. What could we do?

Then the Deaconess Order of the Methodist Church, which had been closed to newcomers for some time, was re-opened again. This time it opened to men as well as women. Denis took a great interest in this, reading all the literature, and after a time of prayer he felt that he was meant to candidate for this Order. So we agreed that there was no point in pursuing the matter of other housing at Cliff until we had a decision about Denis's candidature. The process was lengthy. After initially talking to the Superintendent Minister of our Methodist Circuit, the first step was to meet before the Church Council where we were members. This duly took place and after he explained what the Order was about and his sense of 'call' the vote from the meeting was overwhelmingly in his favour with not one dissension. This was most encouraging.

Denis then contacted the Diaconal Order and, being honest, he decided it was only right to declare his dyslexia. From that point on it became quite difficult as they tried to dissuade him from candidating due to his disability. However we both felt that if he didn't press on with the candidature he would always wonder whether this was a 'call' of God or not. He needed to test the call. An interview with the District Chairman, a saintly man called Revd Brian Rippin, went well and Denis was encouraged to continue. A full day at the Diaconal Order's Headquarters in Birmingham, with myself and our own Minister required to attend, was far more fraught, Denis having to attend an interview with a psychologist. However Denis did get through to what we Methodists call 'the final weekend' when candidates for both the ordained and lay ministries have to attend for a series of formal and informal interviews. Denis returned from the weekend feeling fairly confident that he had done well, and we awaited the results which could change our future for many years to come.

During all of this I had struggled greatly. I was 100% behind Denis's candidature, wanting him to be in the centre of God's will if the Diaconal Order was where God wanted him to be. However I was aware that most if not all of these appointments were in town and city centres. This I did **not** relish at all. I hate the smoke and the smells and the noise, and the hustle and bustle. I offered many prayers to the Lord about it. Even before Denis received the awaited letter with the decision I found that the Lord had completely changed my heart and mind about this, and I had begun to think of and appreciate the benefits of living in a city centre. I knew that only the Lord could have wrought that change in me. Sadly the decision was not what Denis had hoped for. It was God's 'no' to this lay ministry, and we now had to faithfully continue the work He had led us to at Cliff College and the Parish Council. However God had taught me yet another lesson about how He can change hearts and minds when we seek His perfect will and surrender it to Him.

During the time Denis had gone through the process of candidature there had been changes in staffing in the College. Other persons were in positions of higher authority and there had also been changes on the College Committee – persons from outside the College community who were charged with some major decision making. Denis and I decided that we would again put our request to the College to consider that we 'live out', explaining that now Denis had been turned down for the Diaconal Order we were sure that we were meant to remain at Cliff College. In fact we felt it was the Lord's intention that we remain for the rest of Denis's working life. We asked a few close friends to pray about our request. One of these was Mary Mather. Mary was a close friend of my Mum (Irene) and a very prayerful lady. She was one of those few gems of a friend whom one can completely rely on for prayer support. There was no answer to our prayers for some time but we continued to pray. One day Mary rang up and told us that she had been given a picture by the Lord. For those who've never experienced this it usually happens when a person is praying and, with their eyes closed, they see something as if they were seeing with their eyes open. (I have only had this experience once in my life but to this day I do not know what it was meant to convey to me). "Ginny" said Mary excitedly, "I was praying and the Lord gave me a picture for you. It was of you going in through your own front door".

To the reader you may ask 'what was so strange about going in through your own front door?' The entrance to our flat at College was via the College main entrance door (reception) and then up two flights of stairs. Our accommodation was not self-contained with its own front door leading to the outside. So this news from Mary was very exciting although we couldn't fathom out what it could mean. As Denis was still required to live on his job, which meant living in the College building, this was not possible. Perhaps it meant the College would allow us to 'live out'? Perhaps our desire to have a council house would be realised? We had to wait some time before it became clear. Quite some time later Denis and I were summoned to the office of Maurice, the College Administrator. He cut to the chase very quickly. "We'd like to offer you Emmaus" he said, "what do you think about that?" We were quite taken aback for a few moments, and the modern terminology 'gob-smacked' comes to mind as we were quite speechless. 'Emmaus' cottage was away from the College building, down at the bottom of the orchard and near to the Conference Centre and the buildings connected to the College's outreach work.

As the reader may well imagine we were not too long in saying "yes please"! Maurice made it quite clear that Denis would still have the responsibility of dealing with those parts of his work that required him to live on site, such as responding to the fire alarm and his particular responsibilities in that and other areas of work. One of the first things we did on moving into Emmaus was to run telephone extension cables around the rooms of the cottage so that he would always be at the end of the phone in such emergencies and able to fulfil the role required of him. This was indeed God's 'yes' to this longed-for prayer request.

Emmaus had not many years before been converted from a playroom, where the local Playgroup had met, into a cottage. It was on three floors. From the front door on ground level there was a large double bedroom, a large storage room, and an under-the-stairs cloakroom. A few stairs led to a landing where there was a large single bedroom and the bathroom. More stairs led to the living room and the kitchen. This upper floor had wonderful views, different to but every bit as lovely as those from our flat in the College building. The living room looked out onto the large grassed area where the marquee was sited at special times in the College year, and across farmer's fields and up to Curbar and Calver edges – a grit stone edge of approx 1000 feet, popular with tourists and walkers. The kitchen at the back of the property had a dormer window and from it we could see the tops of the apples trees in the orchard. However at night, through that window, the view of the night sky with myriads of stars was just spectacular. Some nights if needing to go up into the kitchen for some tablets, a drink etc, I would gaze for ages at the beauty of our solar system – quite awestruck. The kitchen had been beautifully fitted with very modern units, and the bathroom was fully tiled. Several rooms had been carpeted, so we had no expense there. The cottage had its own little private front garden, and as time went by we were allowed to reclaim some of the uncultivated ground at the bottom of the orchard at the back of the cottage, where we made a quiet and private little garden, enclosed by the dreaded Leylandii! It was an oasis of peace and quiet. We had some very happy times in Emmaus before we had to leave. We had also almost completed full re-decoration prior to having to leave it behind, doing this before I was due to retire when we anticipated having less money to do so. Despite our happiness in this lovely dwelling, and all these efforts to improve it, little did we know that life was about to change yet again and quite drastically.

CHAPTER TWENTY

GOD'S PERFECT TIMING

'There is a time for everything and a season for every purpose under heaven'

(Ecclesiastes 3 : 1)

GOD'S TIMING IS always perfect, and in the time just before and after I retired I was more aware of this than ever before

In summer of 2003 the staff at the College had undergone a pay re-structuring process. During this time Denis, who is quite astute, suspected that all might not be well. Despite what other members of staff said Denis and I kept our own counsel and prepared ourselves for something which, at that time, we were not aware would happen. We just had a feeling that was hard to describe even between ourselves.

It was in September of 2003 that five members of staff, including Denis, received letters of redundancy. We then knew that we had been prepared for this. Their jobs were to go and there was to be a shake up which would create completely new ones. Denis was invited to apply for any which he thought were suitable for him but after studying the full details there were none which would be appropriate. Only one might have been possible but it would have had more unsocial hours than before; working late nights and weekends, and on reduced pay. We could not afford that, especially as there were also to be changes regarding the rent-free housing etc which went with the job.

Having suffered from dreadful migraines which our doctor said were stress-related to Denis's job it didn't take us very long to make an important decision, one which was very carefully prayed over and considered. Denis would take his redundancy package, we would move out and get a Council house, and he would look for a job that was less pressured. Hopefully this· would mean a reduction and eventual cure of the migraines. These came every weekend, so when he wasn't working he was suffering extreme attacks of migraine and never got any rest. When he wasn't having migraine he was 'working his socks off' as the saying goes. We had to get off the treadmill before Denis's health became worse, or (because of a family history of heart-related health problems) even critical. Although we assumed that God would not cause redundancy, nevertheless it was one way in which Denis could be helped to get off the treadmill of health problems.

However, our attempts to seek housing were somewhat frightening and not so cut and dried as we had imagined. We had assumed that because we had put our names down on the Council housing list when we arrived at Cliff in late 1988, this meant we would walk into a

VIRGINIA HAYWOOD

Council property immediately we had need of it. We had assumed as the years went by that this would be at Denis's retirement, as we had latterly felt that Denis's 'calling' was to be at Cliff College until that time. We had felt this very strongly, until the migraines and the stress set in, which then started to cause many doubts and questionings. With regard to housing the reality of the times in which we were living were very different from what we had imagined. It transpired that there were more people in housing need than there were council (or other) properties to rent. We were not in a financial position to buy and never would be, and private rented properties in the Peak National Park were at a premium owing to their high rents. We had been settled into life within or near the Peak District for 15 years and had friends, interests and commitments in that area. Therefore it seemed inappropriate and undesirable to move away; if we did we would be faced with the problem of not being eligible for affordable rented property due to local occupancy clauses.

Initially the local authority was unable to help us, and our attempts to find affordable private rented through Housing Associations was not too fruitful either due to the local occupancy clauses. These meant one had to either be working in the locality, or have a close relative there, or other such local connection clauses. If there were no housing association properties where one was currently living then these clauses certainly ruled out any being available to us further afield. Also, due to my age and the fact we had no children, only old person's property was available to us. This was a blow as we had hoped for a reasonably sized home in which we could comfortably entertain friends, have church fellowship groups, and where we would have room to follow our interests – Denis his studying and me the music and writing I had waited until retirement to take up. The idea of only a one bed roomed old person's flat or bungalow devastated us, and to some extent shattered all our dreams for the future.

As the weeks passed by very much prayer went into this matter of housing. I prayed ardently about my desire for at least a two-bedroom property, that it wouldn't be a flat but if it had to be old person's property then a bungalow. As we had little money I prayed that our recently new and expensive custom made curtains would fit the windows in whatever was eventually offered to us, and that there would be enough storage for all the things we owned. The latter included Denis's enormous library of mostly theological books, and copious amounts of files relating to preaching, studies, and other things we were involved in. Along with prayer we also consulted various organisations and agencies for help and advice about housing but whilst they gave us lots of helpful legal advice it didn't bring the matter of finding a home any nearer. We were getting really desperate.

Round about this time we had a speaker at the Christian Coffee Club in Matlock who, during her testimony, told of the way God had taken care of her housing problems. She offered prayer afterwards for anyone who needed it. I went forward and shared about the housing and during prayer for me she started to speak in tongues, followed by what I now understand was prophecy. I cannot since remember much of that prophecy but what I did feel was the peace that came from that experience. As she spoke in tongues and then said things in English to me I truly had the sense that God cared about the dilemma we were in and that He was at work. I found another of Mum's poems; it seemed appropriate:

Life is full of interest.
It has its ups and downs,
It leads to country places,
To cities and to towns.
It holds its many corners,
The rocky place and smooth,
Its smiling generous people
And those who seem uncouth.
But, Praise the Lord, He trod it,
He knows the way so well,
And as we follow in His way
His praise within can dwell.

We had certainly ridden far and wide, country place and town, to see what kind of dwellings there may be which would suit us, if offered. And there had indeed been the rocky places and the smooth – the places we would like to live, and those we wouldn't. Through these difficulties we did indeed try to praise Him as we trusted Him to work out His plan.

Then one day we got a letter from the local authority to say they had recommended us for a property with a Housing Association. We had given up all hope that any of the applications we had made would come to fruition but in fact this non-Council association now offering to us – Northern Counties Housing Association – just happened to be one we had applied to privately. They had been recommended to us by a friend who lived in one of their properties not too far away, and she thought very highly of them. On talking to one of the staff in the Housing Department at the local authority she said "we are so pleased to be able to recommend you for one of these homes, they are far superior to our Council houses!" The property we were being recommended for was a two-bedroom, category one, sheltered bungalow in a village about eight miles away. What a wonderful answer to prayer!

The wait to view the property seemed interminable and by now we were anxious to see what rooms it had, what sizes, whether our furniture would fit in, whether the curtains would fit (!) how many carpets we would have to buy, what storage space there might be...

After a visit to interview me by a member of the Housing Association we finally received a date to meet up with a Housing Officer and view the property. It was now only a month to the date when Denis would complete his redundancy notice and finish his job and when, realistically, we should vacate the home that went with it. I felt sure that in no way would Cliff College make us move out without a home to go to, but we may have been charged rent etc. The bungalow was on an estate of mixed 'affordable housing' properties – several old people's bungalows, two blocks containing a ground floor and a first floor flat, and several houses which were to rent and others which were shared ownership properties. The bungalow we were shown was in a corner position between three other bungalows and two flats, and from the front looked very pokey and uninteresting. However, first glances can be deceptive. The front door opened into a small porch and then through another door into a decent sized entrance hall. Leading from that were 6 other doors! These led into the main bedroom, the bathroom, the second bedroom, the living room, a storage room, and one was the airing cupboard. The main bedroom was amazing, having floor to ceiling glass fronted fitted wardrobes with sliding doors, the full length of one wall. When we looked at the space in them there was far more than our clothes would ever take, and this was indeed the answer to our prayers for storage space! The bathroom was long and again had a storage cupboard fitted on one wall, giving ample storage for towels and other things. It contained a shower with a seat in it, adapted for a wheelchair user, and had an extra wide door, opening outwards, presumably also for wheelchair use. The second bedroom was a very ample size, suitable for another double bed, and the storage room would be useful to adapt for many purposes, including the siting of the chest freezer we had saved up to buy. The airing cupboard was a more than an adequate size with several shelves for storage.

The Living Room was smaller than we had hoped, although a later visit with measurements showed that we could just about fit our furniture in. The second surprise was the floor to ceiling double glazed glass door and window along the majority of one wall which gave a wonderful open view across the communal gardens to fields and woodlands beyond. We were not overlooked and it seemed that this would be a lovely quiet place to live in. After being at Cliff with constant noise from students, visitors, and major events of the year, Denis's need for complete quiet when suffering migraines, and mine with tension headaches, meant this property and location was ideal.

It looked as if our curtains, recently purchased and fairly expensive, would probably fit, and this did indeed prove to be the case with a very slight and inexpensive adjustment. The kitchen was through a door which opened from the far end of the living room and although a different shape to our kitchen at Cliff seemed to have approximately the same amount of cupboard space and the usual spaces for cooker, washer and a fridge. We very quickly and gratefully signed on the dotted line, paid our first month's rent, and then went for a celebratory cup of coffee and piece of cake at a nearby Garden Centre café before Denis went back to work!

Not long after that Denis became sick with a dreadful virus which put him to bed and feeling terrible. This meant that he was flat on his back and unable to help for most of the time when things were being transferred from our home at Cliff to the new property; when my wonderful 60th birthday party took place (my only party ever in my life); and when all kinds of arrangements had to be made such as buying new carpets, booking the removal men etc were all taking place. How on earth would I cope? Also what about the finance of all this move?

With regard to the latter we had been saving very hard for quite some time and this particular year we had sacrificed our desperately needed annual holiday so we could put the money towards all the expenses involved in moving. However it's very easy to forget that it's far more than just the actual removal van and that there are many peripheral costs involved. Not long before we moved, a very kind person who had become a friend through my Parish Council work had given me a sum of money as a 'love gift' to pay for the actual removal. This friend was a Christian so I had no doubt that this was part of and only the beginning of God's provision for our needs and I was grateful not only to her but to the Lord. My second 'angel of mercy' was my dear friend June. June had worked at Cliff College on the domestic staff and when she retired from work our friendship had deepened. We had spent several years doing our weekly shop together and formed a friendship through the supermarket shopping aisles. When she knew that Denis was ill, and I was so burdened by the amount of work I had to do, she had no hesitation in offering to help in any way she could. Many journeys were spent together, not this time to the local market town and the Supermarket aisles, but backwards and forwards with boxes from Cliff College to our new home some eight miles away.

Then it came to the problems of buying new carpets; how was I to manage without Denis's help? Easygoing man that he is, Denis had no hesitation in suggesting that I go on my own and choose whatever I wished, within our financial means of course. Out of all the drudgery of packing up and removing this was a great pleasure! Fortunately for me before Denis became ill he had measured the floors in the rooms of the bungalow and he had carefully kept all the details. What a blessing that the Lord had provided me with a husband who thought and acted well in advance where the practicalities of life were concerned.

These journeys were a real joy. It wasn't often we had money to splash out on things like new carpets and furniture so I made the most of the days out choosing these, within our limited means, along with the necessary but blissful task of choosing a new dining room suite owing to the lovely old table we had been given collapsing because it had become riddled with woodworm. Despite my problems with converting feet and inches to metres, the salesman in the carpet shop couldn't have been more helpful, and I had nothing to fear about coping. I made several trips to do the choosing and each time the salesman kindly rolled up the carpets to fit into the car boot and away I went to take them to their new home. Owing to the redundancy package we were not so strapped for cash that we couldn't afford some new things that we really needed.

There were many 'angels of mercy' during the transition between our home at Cliff College and the new home and I am often reminded of the words of the hymn 'but His angels here are human, not the shining hosts above'. Amongst them was Peter, a friend and a great confidant. In practical terms he helped Denis to put together a DIY bookcase. However, during the time we were looking for another home and when there were many problems to sort through, he was a source of great help, wisdom, and advice as he helped us sort through a lot of legal problems. I don't know what we would have done without him. Neil, one of Denis's work colleagues, after a long hard day at work travelled all the way down to Nottingham with us in the College van to help us load and unload a very heavy bookcase which had several heavy and fragile glass doors.

In the midst of all this, and despite those initial feelings of misgiving at retiring from my job a month earlier than planned, I realised that it had indeed been the right thing to do. I do believe that the Lord prompted me to do so because He knew what was before us and the need for me to be free. I know that realistically my withdrawal from work was done through a sense of not being able to cope anymore. However I believe there was a certain amount of the Lord's hand in this too. There is a saying ' the Lord will never give you more than He knows you can cope with'. I believe that is very true. In this instance I needed the time and the strength during that month to do all of these things, especially with Denis being so ill in bed.

By the time of removal Denis had just about recovered. The removal men came and were quickly packed up and away, and the unpacking at the other end was soon done. We thought our home at Cliff College was small but when the unpacking started we realised that this one was certainly much smaller. The furniture fitted in very well – we had made sure of that when Denis had made templates of our furniture out of newspaper, putting them on the floor to ensure we could fit everything in where we thought it ought to go. But once the unpacking of the boxes by the removal men started, I quaked inside. They filled every available space in the bungalow that was not covered by furniture, and by the time the removal men left there was hardly room to get into the bathroom and make a passage to the toilet! Boxes were packed in almost to the ceiling! How on earth would we cope? Where would we put everything? We quickly realised that our home at Cliff College had been deceptively larger than this one. There had been an enormous loft space that we had used extensively, and a storage room of a considerable size for a small cottage and we began to realise the extent of the storage space we had left behind and which had been so necessary to us. When packing up we had systematically and ruthlessly gone through all our things and thrown, recycled, or sold much of it. It was hard to believe that we still had such a lot of stuff!

In the days and weeks that followed, and as we gradually sorted ourselves out, we realised anew how important was that seemingly selfish prayer of mine that the Lord would provide us with plenty of storage space. Although what we now had was not what we'd envisaged we did eventually manage to house all our things, and were grateful to the Lord for His provision and His answers to our prayers. How gracious He is in answering prayer for what others would think of as un-necessary requests. I continue to be amazed that the Lord cares about every minute detail of our lives.

CHAPTER TWENTY ONE

THE HARD TIMES

'Take my yoke upon you and learn of Me. . . for my yoke is. . . comfortable, gracious, and pleasant. . . light and easy to be borne'
(Matthew 12: 29-30 Amp)

THE DAYS AND months that followed the move were far from easy. However we knew that, difficult as it had been, we had taken the right decision in Denis accepting redundancy. It is hard to explain to others the dreadful pain and suffering which isn't always apparent to them. Some we met wondered why we had moved away, or why Denis hadn't taken another job at Cliff. There was a sense that we felt we must justify our actions to them, but didn't want to do that nor to run Cliff College down in any way. Although we were really sad at moving away we knew we would value for the rest of our lives all that Cliff College and its people had meant to us. We felt that 'you can take Denis and Virginia out of Cliff but you can never take Cliff out of Denis and Virginia'. We would love it forever for all that it had meant to us.

Also I had got to the bitter end with the Parish Council work and its pressures, and the effect of that and past experiences had an irreversible effect on my health. Not long after the move a Consultant Neurologist finally confirmed that I suffered from 'muscle contraction headaches' – a squeezing of the skeletal muscles that causes a feeling of pressure in the head. It was acknowledged that this was the result of a stress-related illness. According to the Consultant these headaches were made worse by the fact that the very medication given to ease them were now causing 'medication induced headaches'. A vicious circle. Like Paul in the Bible I had many times prayed for healing, but despite prayers from many folk, laying on of hands for healing, etc, they did not go away. Like Paul I felt as if this was my 'thorn in the flesh'. So retirement at 60 and a quiet life, with all that entailed, was very necessary, and I had looked forward to it for a long time.

That was okay for me but Denis was seven years younger than I, with several working years of life to go. He had been sad to leave Cliff College, a place that had meant so much to him and been a part of his life for much longer than the 18 years he had worked there. In our 15 years there as a couple it had come to mean even more. However common-sense had prevailed as Denis knew for a fact that he could not continue with the kind of work he was doing and keep on suffering the severe migraines. After leaving and moving home he 'signed on' and started looking for work. We thought that he would find it easily but as the weeks and months dragged by we became quite despondent. Despite being able to turn his hand to many things Denis had no formal qualifications and the kind of work he was now looking for was not available. He knew that he had to avoid pressured work and long hours that caused and exacerbated the migraines. He loved driving and found it relaxing, and decided that this would be his main aim in looking for work. However that was not so easy either. Many employers were looking for people who would put in an extraordinary amount of unreasonable/unsocial hours, or work during the night time, and Denis knew he could not do this. Throughout his life he had never been able to cope unless he had really early nights, and not long before she died his mother told us that when he was a very young boy he would sleep during the day when others of his age were quite lively. I think this had puzzled her somewhat, but it was a pattern that had continued into adulthood. Some employers wanted someone with a PSV or HGV licence and without these Denis could not get driving work. Also the training costs were enormous, far beyond our financial reach. Denis visited every business in the local village and its surrounds to seek driving or any other suitable work, and then even further afield. Although some of them invited him to leave his name and address, or complete an application form for some unspecified possible future vacancy, nothing came of any of them.

He then started looking for jobs in far distant towns. As he did so, after very careful consideration, we took the massive decision for Denis to take a tax-free lump sum of his Occupational Pension. This meant we could replace our now old and unreliable car with a new reliable one that would enable him to seek work further afield. Living out in the country is far from easy. Public transport is infrequent and either doesn't run to the place you want to go, or doesn't run at the appropriate time. Yet despite buying the car, everything he applied for further afield also came to naught. We didn't know whether it was his age, or his lack of qualifications, or the fact that he was dyslexic, or just because he honestly declared his health problems on application forms. Every door seemed to be closed to him. It was a very stressful and demoralising time and it affected both of us.

Some friends suggested that Denis approach the doctor and ask to be recommended for sickness benefit but it didn't seem right to us. Migraine was not classed as a disability or a long-term illness; it came and went according to pressure and length of working hours. Neither was dyslexia classed as a disability. We had many discussions on the ethics of all this and it was a very testing time as we agonised over the right thing to do. He did get a job 'on trial' for a specified number of weeks as agreed by the Job Centre but the employer was far from honest in stating the hours of work required, saying it was 8:45 am to 4:15 pm. After only 2 or 3 weeks on the job, and working hours far in excess of those agreed and with no extra pay, Denis was getting migraines again. He had no choice but to leave for the sake of his health. When he followed the procedures set down by the Job Centre for leaving the job 'on trial' within a certain period of time he found that, contrary to what the leaflets and the Job Centre had stated, for some inexplicable reason they withdrew his unemployment benefit, despite signing on to look for work again. There was the temptation to ask where was God in all of this but we both tried hard just to keep on trusting Him for our future. There is a verse in the Bible that I once preached on, and at times like this I found really helpful. Jesus said "in the world you shall have tribulation, but be of good cheer I have overcome the world". When we give our lives to Him it doesn't exempt us from the problems of the world; we suffer them just like others. But we do know that whatever we are suffering Jesus is there with us, giving us strength and helping us to cope amidst the struggles.

We were mystified as to what to do next. It was obvious that the migraines were not going to go away as quickly as we had hoped and that there were just not the steady jobs with steady hours. Certainly not those that would ensure Denis a migraine-free existence. After much heart searching, talking, and praying, we agreed that he would continue to take his residual occupational pension and take time out from work, paying Class 3 voluntary contributions to safeguard his future state pension. During the next year we would see whether we could manage financially and whether his health would be better.

Denis continued to do his Diploma Studies (his hobby) that he had started many years before at Cliff College in his spare time out of working hours. He was now able to take his time with them and to enjoy them, and there was always the thought that perhaps one day they might actually lead to a job. One could not imagine what kind of a job, as these were Christian Studies, but we realised that the Lord knew what He was about and He would open a door of opportunity for work for Denis when and if the time was right. In the meantime his studies helped him in many ways, especially his preaching. Throughout this time, when we had taken this difficult decision, I was at peace within myself. It was good not to see Denis suffering constantly with the migraines which had reduced him to tears many times and which were so painful that he metaphorically almost banged his head against the wall in despair. To see him so much better, despite our reduced circumstances, was reward enough for me, and the relief made a difference to my own well-being, and my own headaches decreased in their severity.

After a while Denis started to come with me and my female friends to the Christian Coffee Club in Matlock, which we had been attending for 5 years or so. He really enjoyed the talks and the testimonies given there and began to be built up again in his faith. One needs to understand that leaving a place like Cliff College with its constant flow of wonderful Christians passing through, and the precious conversations of faith, was a great loss to both of us, especially to Denis. As he met and talked with people at the Coffee Club he learnt that the Christian bookshop in the town needed more volunteer helpers. Denis loved books, and had served Cliff College and the Sheffield Methodist District by taking along a bookstall from the College to Synod twice a year, so had relevant experience. So he decided to offer as a volunteer to the Matlock bookshop. Thus began a period of new interest that brought him into contact with many Christians and where he was not only able to serve but also share faith with customers. This began to fill the gap left by Cliff College. Whilst this is my story, once married to Denis it inevitably became linked to his, and what affected Denis affected me too. So although this was Denis's experience it therefore impacted on my life and I had a deep sense of peace that he was doing the right thing, and gratitude to the bookshop and to God for giving Denis this new opportunity to put his faith and his gifts into practice. To know that he was moving in another useful direction made such a difference to my life and to how I felt, and it lifted me up considerably. After a short while Denis was asked if he would become one of the Trustees for the Bookshop Trust, and he was delighted to accept. The Lord was certainly guiding him onwards.

My life also began to take on fresh interests. I engaged in and completed a computer course, which Denis and I did together, and being able to use computer and then the Internet and emails opened up a whole new world in terms of communications, and in monetary savings! I then had the opportunity to do volunteer work for the Housing Association of which we were tenants. It is a wonderful organisation that really values its tenants and offers all manner of ways of becoming involved. I opted to become a member of the Residents Council and it was a decision I never regretted. Much of what I had learnt over the years came into play and I began to enjoy this new freedom to make a difference to other people's lives in unexpected ways. The Housing Association was generous in reimbursing the travel costs of attending the meetings and even providing us with lunch and tea/coffee snacks. In addition some of the conference venues were just superb. I never envisaged the privileges I would enjoy just for being a volunteer. It was good to feel that after an important job of work as a Parish Clerk I again had a role to play and a valuable contribution to make. Due to Denis being at home with me retirement had not really taken the path I anticipated and planned. I had to let go of many dreams, and many adjustments had to be made between us, and this was quite difficult. However, life was turning out to be most interesting. I even found at one of our landlord's meetings that some of the folk there were Christians and was asked to pray for some of their relatives. Surely God's Hand was in this.

Another volunteer interest, not unconnected, was one that had surfaced while I was still working as a Parish Clerk. Among the many Parish Council papers which popped through my letter box down the years was one for the public notice-board seeking people interested in an Affordable Housing Working Group. The idea of being part of it grabbed me when it arrived but I was so very busy with my work that it had to be put to one side. Once we had moved home, and particularly after the experiences of our search for a home and the concerns for affordable housing this had evoked, I remembered this organisation and started to attend their meetings. Not only did I again feel I had a distinct contribution to make but I even met a Christian there also. Again it was good to know that there were Christian links to be made away from the church, and people who needed prayer outside the walls of the church.

After spending fifteen years living in a Christian College I was reminded sharply of the fact that there are many Christians living and working away from church situations who are no less effective in their witness than those in ordained ministry. Some Christians think that unless they are doing the Lord's work in an ordained or lay ministry they are not doing anything for Christ. However there is a wide world outside of the church and it needs its Christians every bit as or perhaps even more than the church itself.

The day I was asked by a Residents Council member to pray for her son who was training for the Methodist Ministry I began to feel I was doing what God wanted me to do in the place He wanted me to do it. I believed that wherever I was serving, in whatever role, He could put me in touch with the people He needed me to meet, for His purpose. The work we do for Him does not have to be spectacular; we do not always have to be 'up front'; but we need to be willing to be where He wants to place us and sometimes to take the humbler tasks, whatever those are. As time went by the wonderful Yamaha keyboard that we had bought several years earlier also became a useful tool in the service of the Lord as I started to take it to churches without an organist. Revd David Cooper, a Methodist Minister who had built his own portable organ to use in just such purposes, and had recorded the whole of the Methodist hymn book 'Hymns and

Psalms', had let us have a complete set of these disks for a very small cost. This was because we had been at Cliff College, a place which was very close to his heart. These disks were very useful in helping provide music for churches, especially as I couldn't play the keyboard.

The hard times continued. There was never much money to go round but we learnt to cope and to 'cut our coat according to our cloth' as the old saying goes. In the early days of our marriage we had to learn to manage on little and had always felt this would stand us in good stead for the future. Money was saved on some things and put towards others we wanted or needed. The money paid out for a second-hand computer from Cliff College's leaving gift to Denis was the start of something completely new to us and which would prove so beneficial. A small monthly payment to get onto the Internet and use email facilities also opened up a whole new world to us. Via websites we learnt much about how to use our money more effectively, how to make savings on things we needed, and how to communicate with friends via emails. This saved us a tremendous amount of money on paper, envelopes, postage and telephone calls. Although our voluntary work was unpaid our travel expenses were refunded and in this way the Lord ensured that our needs were always met.

We didn't get large amounts of money fluttering down as it were 'from heaven' but we knew where our provision came from and to whom we owed thanks and praise. We remembered the words of the sermon at our marriage ceremony, from Luke's Gospel, chapter 12, verses 22cf. When Denis received a small legacy on his mother's death, it just about covered the cost of the replacement cooker and other kitchen equipment that we desperately needed. When the

2 year-old car we had bought became inadequate to carry the equipment we needed in the Lord's service, even that was taken care of. We found out the value of our car from the kind people we bought it from, we read up advice on 'bargaining' and we sent email prayer requests round some friends. Again there were no large pots of money floating down from heaven but things did happen which enabled us to buy a suitable car albeit a few years older. People prayed – thank God for praying friends – and one sent us a moderate cheque towards the cost. We bargained with the dealer where we saw a suitable vehicle. And, miracle of miracles, and despite his reluctance to give us the sum we wanted for ours in part exchange, after talking to his boss the salesman did just that! More than that he then offered to do the full 10,000 mile service on the car for free. This meant that the money we had budgeted for a service on our present car that year would not be needed. The £300 saving could go towards the balance of the purchase price for this other car. Then having surfed the web to look at Car Insurance deals we got about 50 quotes, some of which were incredibly low. However, my wise husband insisted that we go back to our Insurance Brokers to see what they could do, as he was afraid that the cheap quotes might not be as good as they seemed. He told the Insurance Broker the quotes we had found and although the car we were buying had a larger engine our Brokers got us another quote from our present Insurer which was £100 cheaper but with all the same safeguards in place! So we had another £100 towards the cost of our "new" car. And so it went on, little by little, and by the time we had done the deal we only had 50p to find from our fairly small savings.

Not only this but it turned out that the car we were

buying was a motability car and it was amazing. I had started to suffer with arthritis in the last few years and it was becoming steadily worse. It was not helped by getting into the low seat of our other car. The car we were changing to was higher, and the seats bigger and not so low slung. The driver's seat was adjustable so one could raise it, and even adjust a section of the back of the seat to create a small bump in one's lumbar region. It was amazing and from the first time I sat in it I knew this was car was going to help my condition tremendously. Little did I know at that time that within just a few short months a definite diagnosis of osteoarthritis would be confirmed and my condition would accelerate. At the time this book is being written there is concern about how we will afford the petrol to run the car, but I need to remember what God through Jesus has done in both our lives so far, and I need to trust Him completely for those needs.

Little by little, despite the difficulties of the last two years, the Lord was providing for our needs and was opening up new ways of service and interest for both of us, and we rejoiced at His love and His gracious provision for us.

CHAPTER TWENTY TWO

BACK TO THE FUTURE

**'Fix these words of mine in your hearts and minds . . .
teach them to your children. . .so that your days and
the days of your children may be many in the land. . .as
many as the days that the heavens are abov e the earth**

(Deuteronomy Chapter 11: 18-21)

**'. . . what we have heard and known, what our
fathers have told us, we will not hide... from their
children; we will tell the next generation the
praiseworthy deeds of the Lord, His power, and the
wonders He has done' (Psalm 78: 3-4)**

BACK TO THE future? Yes indeed, for if it were not for the past
– its experiences and its people – I would not be where I am
today. The film 'Back to the Future' is about a boy who was
catapulted back to the past and then the future several times

via a time machine. As a result of what happened in those experiences of time travel he was able to alter the present and the future for the better. This film and its two sequences were a wonderful piece of fiction but we're not yet advanced to the point where scientists can give us time travel, although I understand some have actually talked about its possibility in the future. But we don't need time travel to ensure that the past has a positive effect on the future. So this is about looking back in time to see what shaped the future – the time leading up to the present in which I now stand, and the things which may well shape the future before me.

Throughout my story you have seen how I have given little glimpses back into the past, as those were relevant to my story. You have read my story from conversion to Christ onwards, and the amazing things that happened to me through the people God brought into my life as part of His plan during that time. This final part of my story includes people who were there from birth right up to my conversion, and people and experiences throughout my life, not yet mentioned but which have shaped my life. My story would be incomplete without them.

The Bible relates many examples of looking back to the past. It's important to realise that not all of our looking back is bad, like the sad fate of Lot's wife in Genesis Chapter 20, verse 26, when she was turned into a pillar of salt for doing so. There are, of course, implications if we do the wrong thing in life or wilfully disobey God, just as doing wrong will always have its own consequences. But if we then try our best to put things right again, sometimes saying sorry, which for Christians is repentance, we may well find that the Lord will use the bad things for good effect – turning them around completely.

Most if not all of my looking back is to those things which were good and fruitful in my life. The scripture quote from Deuteronomy in the title of this chapter is a reminder that the Israelites were admonished to remember the laws which God gave to them so that they would live good and upright lives which were pleasing to Him. It was also a plea to remember the many and wonderful things which the Lord had done for them and to pass on these remembrances to their children, and their children's children, and future generations. The psalmist also recognised the need to pass on to future generations the wonderful deeds of the Lord. This is because what happened in the past could make a difference to the future.

For Christians in today's world it is also about remembering all that God has done for each one of us, and then using them for good purpose, as God guides. As a result much of my looking back has to do with the people who crossed my path in life and through whom I was guided to accept Jesus Christ, the crucified, risen and exalted Lord, as my Saviour. The people I mention were like pointers along the way – guide posts on a journey to a given destination which is part of my ongoing Christian life today. The journey is an earthly one but its destination is a heavenly city.

The first pointer was my mother, Barbara. As a young child I saw her many times kneeling at her bedside in prayer and I have no doubt that some of her prayers would be for me, especially as she had given birth to me at the age of forty-two. As my Father was several years older than her, by the time I reached young adulthood they would have been more the age of grandparents to me. This could have caused them some concern and maybe some of her prayers for me related to this. She also set an example by faithfully attending her local Anglican Church, often despite failing health and increasing difficulty getting up and down the steep hill where we lived because of arthritis in her limbs. Although my Father did not profess a Christian faith or attend church, he did often talk about the days when as a youngster he used to pump the bellows for the local church organ. Despite not going to church with my mother he never showed any signs of resenting her doing so. Although he never gave me any religious instruction, my father was a generous-hearted, extremely kind and very gentle man, never raised his voice to anyone, and absolutely adored my mother. Whenever I think of God as 'Father' I am helped by the good example of fatherhood set before me by Norman, my human father. These were good seeds that my parents sowed for me in those very early days.

When I was eleven years old my parents sadly had no option but to place me in a children's home for a few years until I left school at fifteen. My mother was not a well lady and I only found out from my family doctor many years after she had passed away that she occasionally had to go into the local mental hospital for electric shock treatment. She was not mentally ill, in fact was a very normal but quiet, kind and intelligent person, but I now realise that in those days people who suffered from depression were often given electric shock treatment. Maybe depression was her problem; I shall never know. However there was a good side to being at the children's home for it was there that I met the second person who became my pointer along the way to Jesus Christ.

As children in the Home we attended the Anglican church in the nearby village. This was Wentworth, halfway between Barnsley and Rotherham in South Yorkshire. The children's home was in a lovely old house in beautiful grounds and surrounded by countryside, and we were really very privileged to be there. We probably didn't think so at the time but looking back it was a character-building time for me. One of the Lay Readers at the church, Mr Tiptaft, also led the Sunday School. He was such a kind and gentle man and we all loved him. He obviously had a very good job and one assumed he was wealthy as he owned either a Rolls Royce or a Bentley. Often when some of us were waiting at the bottom of the lane below the Children's Home to catch a bus to go into the village, he would stop and give us a ride in his car!

One Sunday whilst in Sunday School, I and Susan, one of the other girls in the Home, asked Mr Tiptaft what one had to do to receive Jesus Christ. I believe it was just curiosity for us rather than an actual desire to receive Jesus, but Mr Tiptaft obviously thought differently and with great delight immediately led us to the altar and prayed with us to receive Christ. Word soon got round about this and the staff at the Home were delighted, as were some of the teachers at the comprehensive school we attended a few miles away. Many of them kept saying there was a change in me, although I didn't feel there was. However, for all of the years after that and until he died, Mr Tiptaft kept in touch with me through letters. He always ended his letters with the phrase 'keep on keeping on'. Words of encouragement to keep pursuing the goal – a little like Paul's words to Timothy in the Bible. When he knew that I had become a Methodist Local Preacher he was absolutely delighted and it was such a joy to actually share faith with him through my letters, in a way I had never been able to until about my early to mid forties.

Of great significance in my spiritual journey to Christ was one of the staff in the Home, Caroline Lund. We were allowed to call her Auntie Caroline and we all adored her. There was no doubt that she was a Christian, and we were certainly all made aware of it! In that sense she was a great evangelist!

We often used to go for walks in the countryside around the Home, accompanied by a member of staff, frequently Auntie Caroline. These were fun times. She was adorable and as we walked she would teach us Christian choruses and we would sing along together. I remember the lovely film 'The Inn of the sixth Happiness' which was about the missionary Gladys Aylward. During her time in China Gladys undertook the brave act of leading a very large group of children up and over the mountains, away from the war and into safety. They also sang as they walked, and our time spent walking the countryside of South Yorkshire, loudly singing Christian choruses with Auntie Caroline, was reminiscent of that. Auntie Caroline had a daughter who was a missionary in Brazil and she would often relate stories about what her daughter was doing. Many years later, when I was one of the group of teenagers at the Methodist Church in Holmfirth, Auntie Caroline, with whom I was still in touch, came along to Irene and Joe's home to the Christian Endeavour Group we held there and spoke about her daughter's work.

One of the teachers in the comprehensive school we attended was Miss Charlesworth, the Scripture Teacher. When she heard about Susan and I going forward for an 'altar call' so to speak, she asked if I would like extra lessons. Bless her she actually gave up many of her lunch-breaks to sit and explain the Scriptures to me, and I remember with delight and gratitude those times spent quietly in her classroom, just the two of us, pouring over the Bible. I do not remember her doing this for other pupils. What dedication that was and how fondly I remember her.

Much later still, during my first marriage, one of the jobs I had was with James and Betty Robinson, in a village just outside Huddersfield. The job was to be a mother's help for their three children and to do part-time work in the office. James ran a busy garage along with a taxi business, although I wasn't aware of the latter when I went for the interview. I loved helping with the children, Heather aged about 3 years old, and Philip and David a few years older. As always my great love was office work and that was enjoyable too. James' office was a little wooden hut at the back of his garage with a view right across the valley. It was a lovely situation in which to work. However it wasn't long before I got roped in to help with the taxi driving. I had only just passed my driving test and it quickly became apparent that they were always short of drivers. I must admit to being very reticent at first but it wasn't long before I enjoyed that part of the work almost more than anything else. It was during that time that things in my marriage started to go wrong and although I never talked about it, just being in the presence of James and Betty and the atmosphere of their home was of great help to me. Their home, although my place of work, was like a refuge during stormy times. They were Christians and although they did not shout it from the housetops their whole manner, the way they were with people, the way they treated them, and their business ethics, all spoke volumes. Looking back I realise that they were being used as yet another pointer on the way to Christ.

In recent years other people who have been a great help and influence have been those of the Wesley Fellowship to which Denis and I belong, and in particular the kindness and friendship of its members and the preaching and leadership of Revd Dr Herbert McGonigle. Amongst these people I have found a fellowship and a scriptural teaching the like of which I hadn't experienced for several years. Although the fellowship is made up of people of several Christian denominations the majority of them tend to be from the Church of the Nazarene. They remind me of the folk of the Wesleyan Methodist church I first joined way back in my late teens. The teaching and preaching of Dr McGonigle is second to none and both Denis and I feel completely re-vitalised in every way each time we meet with them.

One of the main pointers along my way to Christ was there both before and after some of those already mentioned above, and she seems an appropriate person to end this section of my final chapter. In my mid to late teens Susan, a friend from the Anglican Church I attended, took me along to the Methodist Church in nearby Holmfirth, the town where I was born. I so loved the extempore prayer and the joyous and hearty singing which was so different from the fairly staid Anglican services I was used to. Although confirmed into the Anglican Church it wasn't long before I chose to become a Methodist member. It was there that I met Irene Hogley (the person you have already read so much about) and her husband Joe, and their children. Irene and Joe ran the Youth Club in the Chapel, a Christian Endeavour Group in their home, and were both Local Preachers. Joe also allowed us young ones to meet on a Sunday evening after Church in a room above his painting and decorating shop. The meeting was called 'squash'! I've never quite understood why – not exactly any religious connotation – but think it was because it was a small room and we were squashed in! I also remember the wonderful time the 'squash' group had when, along with another couple of their adult friends, Irene and Joe took us all on holiday on the Norfolk Broads – boys on one boat, girls on another, and the adults on the third boat! Irene and Joe's love for young people made a tremendous impact on us all and many of us kept in touch for years afterwards.

When in later years my first marriage failed and, for a while, I had no home to go to, as you know from earlier chapters Irene and Joe took me into their home, cared for me, loved me and helped me get my life back together. It was during my time with them that I finally came to know Jesus Christ as my risen and living Lord, my Saviour. It was then that Irene told me that all down the years she had never failed to keep on praying for all of us young people, even though many of us had moved far away. She said that she counted it a privilege to see me 'born again' whilst actually living with them. For my part I counted it a privilege to have received such faithful and constant prayer from her over so many years, resulting in my finally finding and accepting Jesus Christ as my risen Lord and Saviour. I also repeat my earlier part of the story that during this time the people of the Prayer and Bible Study Fellowship in Bramhope, to which Irene and Joe took me, also had a very large part to play in my 'coming to Christ'. I will never ever forget them or the wonderful times I had with them. Their exposition of the Bible, in an informal and loving setting, really opened up the Scriptures to me and helped me to know that Jesus was alive.

So the past had a very definite and important role in my life, and the people I met along the way were indeed God's pointers – like sign posts along the road. Despite the fact that sometimes I misread the pointers, or deliberately and wilfully chose to go the wrong way, these people (these pointers) were always in place just waiting to show me the right way. Not only that but the words they spoke and wrote, and the way they acted – the kind of people they were – were seeds planted in my heart and mind, watered and helped to growth by the Lord Himself, at the right moment in time.

However, the remembering, the looking back, is also much more than about people, it's also about experiences. We are moulded into what we finally become by so many things, and our experiences in life are also part and parcel of this moulding.

Certainly my experiences working at 'Moorlands' played a very large part in shaping me as a Christian. During the periods of the year when we had no Host and Hostess one of my roles was to lead morning and evening prayers. This was a great privilege and also a great joy. I found my inspiration for these devotional times from so many things. Some came from the world around us, especially in such a lovely part of God's creation, and I marvelled at how much inspiration could be found for small talks and prayers from what I saw day by day. Just as Jesus drew on the everyday things around Him when He talked to His disciples and to the crowds, so I too found much in the everyday world to draw people's attention to Him.

Then there was the fellowship with other Christians, day in, day out. What a privilege and a joy that was, too. We walked the walks, long or short, and conversations of faith flowed freely as people shared their innermost thoughts, their concerns, their requests for and their answers to prayer. As both guests and staff shared their personal concerns with me I felt prompted to follow the advice of a well-known Christian writer and I started the prayer journal that you read about in an earlier chapter. It was a joy to read through it again and see how faithfully and wisely God had answered prayers. So during this time not only were rich relationships formed but I became part of this wide circle of Christians learning from each other. This sharing together was so very enriching, and this and God's teaching me about prayer all helped to form me in my Christian life.

My time at Cliff College with Denis was different but similar to this. There I met with an even wider diversity of people and, like 'Moorlands', not all were of the Methodist tradition and not all from Great Britain. Here I learnt several things:

- to value and respect the Christian traditions from which all came, with their diversity of ways of worship and of viewpoints.

- that although we all have our different viewpoints on Christian theology, and our own treasured denominations and ways of worshipping, we can still interact with each other and learn from each other.

- to value those of the Christian faith who came from other countries, particularly the African continent, and found they had a great deal to teach us.

- Most of all, that above and beyond our individual cherished Christian traditions what really mattered was that we all believed that Jesus Christ was the Son of God, that He died on the cross of Calvary for our sins, and rose again to sit in Heaven with His Father where He lives for ever to intercede for us (John Chapter 3, verse 16 cf).

Cliff College foreign students after Graduation ceremony

It was a privilege that those who were on staff, and we their families, could join in so many wonderful times of worship at different events in the College year, along with students and visitors. There were the three great events of the College year. One was 'Celebration Weekend' (the anniversary of the College), another was Derwent Convention Week, and thirdly the College Graduation. Each of these afforded us wonderful times of Bible Study from great scholars of the Bible, and great and joyful tent meetings led by our own very able Evangelistic Team, along with a variety of speakers from different denominations and from various countries.

The Evangelistic Team I remember in particular and shall do so for a long time as their gifts and graces were used not only throughout the year but at these special times. I remember in particular Alf Waite; Greg and Shirley Alexander, Elaine Jones, Carole Thomas and Mark Chambers, whose leading of worship in tent meetings lifted one to great spiritual heights of joy, and they helped me to grow.

I could never say that I was overloaded with worship – it was so wonderful and such a privilege to have so much of it and to be a part of it. I have fond memories of Rev Dr Bill (William) Davies as Principal. During his time at Cliff, and during tent meetings, I experienced again what I had seen and heard at St Matthias' church at Headingley: singing in tongues – the most melodious sound one could experience on earth. This was a time when I began to understand and experience the gifts of the Spirit. In worship with others I experienced the most vibrant and uplifting worship to God; saw and heard the gifts of the Spirit poured out in meetings as people spoke in tongues, and as others interpreted those messages; and people being healed as hands were laid on them and prayers spoken over them.

There were also many Conferences which as staff and families we were privileged to attend, and again these were times of great uplifting, and tremendous spiritual learning curves. I was blessed many times as I listened to people like Revd Dr Colin Morris, Joyce Huggett, Revd Dr Donald English, and many others. Through them I heard the most wonderful expositions of Biblical passages or was led in prayerful contemplation. My heart lifts even to this day as I remember the impact of my time spent at Cliff College.

The College Graduation was also a very uplifting time when students and others were invited to step onto the platform and share their testimonies of what God had done for them. Time and again we heard the most wonderful stories of how God had called them there and sometimes resourced them, and how He had challenged and changed them. What came out most clearly was that He had 'raised them up' in ways beyond their wildest imaginings and enabled them to do things they could never have comprehended.

Also very special were the times when I was privileged to preach and lead worship in the College chapel. It is always a great privilege to preach God's word but doing so in the chapel with students and staff was one of my most encouraging experiences. Singing was robust – whether it was traditional hymns or modern worship songs – and students were always willing to take part in the services. Most of all they were attentive throughout, and always had positive remarks about the sermon preached. I was always very conscious of God's presence in those services and most grateful to Dr Davies the Principal for allowing me this privilege.

It is very important that we look back and see how God led us into the present. As Christians we do that on a fairly regular basis. Each year at Christmas we celebrate by looking back to the birth of Jesus and remember how God deigned to come to earth, to take human flesh in the form of a baby and to grow up into a human life which would shape this world for all time. We then look back each Easter and remember how Jesus followed the path set before Him which led to the cross at Calvary, where He died to take away our sins and to free from sin all who would turn to Him, to receive everlasting life. At Pentecost we look back on the time when God poured out His Holy Spirit on thousands of believers and gave them the power to speak and to heal in Jesus name, and we recognize that this outpouring has changed the lives of millions as they have accepted the promise of eternal life with Jesus. And on a regular basis in our different church traditions the Sacrament reminds us that Jesus told us to "do this in remembrance of me".

We look back in order to see what led us into this future in which we now stand. This is a future that has its ups and downs, for Jesus never promised us it would be free from difficulties. He never said that Christians would be exempt from the trials which beset those who are not in Christ. Jesus was a realist and so He promised that if we stepped into the future with Him He would be with us all the way, helping us, comforting us, giving us strength to endure – being constantly at our side, even in the darkest and most difficult moments in our lives.

So I look back and I thank God that He revealed Himself to me through so many people along life's pathway, and through so many enriching experiences. Most of all I thank Him for showing me that even the humblest and most ordinary of His children can be raised up to a new life. Preaching once from Psalm 40 there were three things in particular which stood out to me. They were that...

- The Lord heard my cry (He is ever present to hear when we call to Him)

- That He lifted me (He raised me out of my sinfulness to a new life)

- He set me in a firm place (the place which is certainty in His presence and His love)

Thanks be to God! He raised me up!

* * * * * * * * * * * * * * * * * * *

You raised me up so I can stand on mountains,
You raised me up to walk on stormy seas,
I am so strong when I am on your shoulders,
You raise me up to more than I can be.
* * * * * * * * * * * * * * * * *

Those who hope in the Lord will renew their strength.
They will soar on wings like eagles;
They will run and not grow weary,
They will walk and not be faint.

(Isaiah 40 : 31)

ISBN 1425126665-0

9 781425 126650